GLASS
AT THE
FITZWILLIAM
MUSEUM

171

GLASS
AT THE
FITZWILLIAM
MUSEUM

CAMBRIDGE UNIVERSITY PRESS

CAMBRIDGE

LONDON · NEW YORK · MELBOURNE

CONTENTS

PREFACE — *page* 5

ABBREVIATIONS AND OTHER INFORMATION — 7

PART I THE ANCIENT WORLD — 11

MESOPOTAMIA — 11

EGYPT — 12
  New Kingdom jewellery and inlays: p. 12. *Toilet vessels:* p. 13. *Sculpture:* p. 15. *Inlays of 11th–1st centuries BC:* p. 15. *Amulets:* p. 16.

OTHER REGIONS UP TO THE ADVENT OF GLASS-BLOWING — 19
  Graeco-Phoenician core-glass: p. 19. *Hellenistic and Early Roman moulded clear glass:* p. 22. *Millefiori and banded glass:* p. 24. *Mosaic glass:* p. 26. *Ancient seals:* p. 30.

EARLY SYRIAN BLOWN GLASS — 31
  Mould-blown: p. 31. *Free-blown:* p. 33.

ROME AND THE WESTERN PROVINCES — 35

HELLENISTIC AND ROMAN JEWELLERY — 42

THE EASTERN PROVINCES OF THE ROMAN EMPIRE — 46
  Egypt: p. 46. *The Danube region:* p. 48. *Palestine:* p. 48. *Syria:* p. 49.

THE DARK AGES — 54
  The East Mediterranean: p. 54. *Western Europe:* p. 56.

PART II THE ORIENT — 59

CHINA — 59

ISLAM — 61

PART III EUROPE FROM THE RENAISSANCE THROUGH THE 17TH CENTURY — 66

VENICE AND NORTHERN EUROPE — 66

ENGLAND — 75

PART IV THE 18TH AND EARLY 19TH CENTURIES — 87

ENGLAND AND IRELAND — 87
  Stem types: p. 87. *Bottles, decanters and jugs:* p. 91. *Coloured and gilded glass:* p. 92. *Enamelling:* p. 96. *Engraved glass:* p. 101. *Irish glass:* p. 106. *'Lynn' glass:* p. 110.

THE CONTINENT — 114
  Engraved glass: p. 114. *Other glass:* p. 118.

PART V THE 19TH AND 20TH CENTURIES — 120

PREFACE

Glassworking from the 15th century BC to the present is the theme of this exhibition. The University's collections in the Fitzwilliam Museum and in the Museum of Archaeology and Ethnology, regarded together, mirror well the history of glass, with the conspicuous but hardly surprising exception of medieval glass. We are glad to be able to exhibit in the Adeane Gallery of the Fitzwilliam a wide selection of our glass taken over the whole range of our holdings, promptly and generously supplemented by significant loans from the Museum of Archaeology and Ethnology which represent vessel production between the 6th century BC and the 7th century AD. A list of these loans is appended. Thanks to Major Raymond Ades we are able to show also his 14th century Islamic sprinkler bottle, a treasured loan to us since 1948, the centenary of our opening to the public.

The purchase of a substantial part of the Cesnola collection in 1876 was the start of our collection of ancient glass. That consisted of vessels excavated in various parts of Cyprus, among them the important Syrian pieces now exhibited. Further glass from the same area was added by several gifts of the Cyprus Exploration Fund, the extensive finds from Paphos received in 1888 being particularly notable. More was given by Sir Henry Bulwer from 1892 onwards. To this nucleus, the Museum's main body of Palestinian glass was joined by the gift of M. Sykes in 1902. Successive benefactions from Dr G. F. Rogers, and a bequest received from E. Towry Whyte in 1932, brought us both Graeco-Roman and Egyptian glass. Meanwhile a long succession of finds presented by the British School of Archaeology in Egypt and by the Egypt Exploration Society had been building up an interesting array of documented Egyptian glass. G. D. Hornblower's Egyptian collection, given in 1939, was especially rich in glass and glazed wares. Yet by far the most important source for Egyptian glass in the Fitzwilliam has been the huge collection formed by R. G. Gayer-Anderson, which was presented in 1943. Twelve years later Sir William Elderton added his smaller but interesting range of Syrian and Palestinian glass. The most recent gift included in this exhibition is of early Mesopotamian glass received from the British School of Archaeology in Iraq in 1977.

Our Roman glass is thus largely drawn from the eastern provinces of the Empire. Fortunately we have been able to borrow freely from the Museum of Archaeology and Ethnology, where the glasswork of the western provinces is well represented. Their collections have developed from those of the Cambridge Antiquarian Society, originating in the main from a succession of local finds augmented by some larger and more widely based private collections, and outstandingly by the gift of Dr J. Barratt in 1886 and the bequest of W. K. Foster in 1891. However, by far the greatest benefaction in ancient glass at the Museum of Archaeology and Ethnology consisted of an extensive series of gifts of diverse provenance from M. F. Ransom, culminating in his bequest of 1923. Lord Braybrooke's collection, most from Britain, but partly Mediterranean, was bought for the Museum in 1948; and an interesting range of Roman and Coptic glass from Egypt was given by J. W. Fell in 1966. Local finds continue; and they include the splendid beaker of Saxon date, which was unearthed in June 1977 by road-works on the A604, near the turn-off to Dry Drayton.

In 1912, with the bequest of Charles Brinsley Marlay, came the bulk of our collection of European continental glass. The Marlay Bequest, especially rich in Venetian and *façon de Venise* vessels, brought also engraved and enamelled glass. Not until the early 1930s, however, were we presented with our first English ware of consequence. Then came the gift of the J. C. Varty-Smith collection by his sisters, and the bequest of the Rev. A. V. Valentine Richards. In the same period Mrs W. D. Dickson, one of the early members of The Glass Circle, made us fine presents of her European glass, continental as well as English and Irish.

The Oriental collections were enriched by the bequest in 1938 of Cecil Byas's collection of snuff bottles of the 18th, 19th and 20th centuries, and by Oscar Raphael's bequest in 1941 of Chinese beads and amulets of the Han and T'ang Dynasties. This material was amplified by Chinese glass from the Ch'ing Dynasty, bequeathed in 1951 by R. F. Lambe. In 1948, in celebration of our centenary as a public museum, we were presented by the National Art-Collections Fund with the mosque lamp of the mid 14th century, a magnificent object which in 1976 we loaned to the Hayward Gallery exhibition in celebration of The World of Islam Festival.

Since 1961 major acquisitions have strengthened our holdings of English and Irish glass. Donald Beves, after some hesitation about the public desirability of dividing what he had bought, left us the whole of the most distinguished private collection of its kind then extant, more than 500 well-chosen objects. They include examples of George Ravenscroft's manufacture, as well as many other 17th century English glasses; an impressive group of 18th century enamelled glasses attributed to the Beilby family, including a goblet signed by William Beilby; and a splendid range of material spanning the 18th century and illustrative of British table-glass during its phase of most independent development.

In 1967 the grant-in-aid fund administered by the Victoria and Albert Museum enabled us to purchase the Verzelini goblet of 1578, thereby extending with *éclat* the chronological boundary of our holdings of English glass to the last quarter of the 16th century.

In 1975 the gift of Miss E. H. Bolitho, through the Friends of the Fitzwilliam, brought us over 150 fine pieces of the 18th and 19th centuries, chiefly English and Irish, collected by her brother-in-law, Ivan Napier, who was, like Mrs Dickson and Mr Beves, a member of The Glass Circle. The Napier collection complements our previous holdings most satisfactorily, being strong in 'Lynn' glass and in cut glass of the early 19th century.

In the 1970s we have used the stringently limited means at our disposal to add pieces of ancient glass, of European continental glass from the mid 18th century onwards, and especially of British glass from the late 19th and from the 20th centuries. Our holdings are in most other respects sufficiently remarkable to make their being made more nearly comprehensive an enjoyable obligation.

It is gratifying that this exhibition in Cambridge is not only inter-departmental within the Fitzwilliam, involving the staff of the Department of Applied Arts, of the Department of Antiquities, and of the Department of Coins and Medals, but also inter-museum within the University. We appreciate the cooperation of the Committee and Staff of the Museum of Archaeology and Ethnology, and especially at a distracting moment of their reorganisation of their own Museum. Miss M. D. Cra'ster has been of frequent help to us there. The greater part of the catalogue, which the active support of the Syndics of the University Press has made possible, has been written by Mrs B. K. Schnitzer: but the sections dealing with glass down to the 7th century AD, have been written by Miss J. D. Bourriau, Miss J. E. A. Liversidge and Mr R. V. Nicholls, with assistance on the Frankish glass from Dr Catherine Hills; while the account of the Islamic weights, stamps and tokens has been contributed by Mr A. H. Morton. Inscriptions on the mosque lamp and on the Islamic sprinkler have been translated by Miss M. Bayani. The ancient glass has benefited from conservation work by Mr N. C. Rayner and Mr F. A. Rookes. Volunteers have laboured in both museums to assist its documentation: Mr Michael Good, Miss Janet Gruber, Miss Nita Krevans and Miss Jennifer Wood. Within the Fitzwilliam's Department of Applied Arts, Mr R. A. Crighton has given specialist advice and Mr J. Lister technical assistance. The photographs are all by Mr F. Kenworthy, apart from those of the seals and weights, which are by our Department of

Coins and Medals. In preparing the catalogue, the authors made extensive use of an earlier photographic record of all the ancient glass compiled by Mr R. D. Stretch. Mrs E. Pandey and Miss J. Williams typed the manuscript. To all these and to the editors and designer of the Cambridge University Press we are grateful.

Those concerned in preparing this exhibition and its catalogue have received invaluable advice outside the University from Dr D. B. Harden and from Mr R. J. Charleston. We owe these two pundits special thanks for their gifts of time and attention.

MICHAEL JAFFÉ
Director

ABBREVIATIONS AND OTHER INFORMATION

Unless otherwise specified, all items in this catalogue belong to the Fitzwilliam Museum. The glass included represents only a limited selection from the University collections in the Fitzwilliam itself and in the Museum of Archaeology and Ethnology, but the selection has been made as varied as possible.

GENERAL ABBREVIATIONS

D: diameter   H: height   L: length   Th: thickness   W: width   cm: centimetres   Coll.: Collection ed.: editor or edition

JOURNALS

AJ	*Antiquaries Journal* (London, 1921 f.)
ArchJ	*Archaeological Journal* (London, 1844 f.)
BMQ	*British Museum Quarterly* (London, 1926–73)
CASP	*Cambridge Antiquarian Society Quarto Publications* (various series)
Conn	*The Connoisseur* (London, 1901 f.)
JEA	*Journal of Egyptian Archaeology* (London, 1914 f.)
JGS	*Journal of Glass Studies* (Corning, New York, 1959 f.)
JRS	*Journal of Roman Studies* (London, 1911 f.)
PCAS	*Proceedings of Cambridge Antiquarian Society* (Cambridge, current series 1935 f.)
QDAP	*Quarterly of Department of Antiquities in Palestine* (Jerusalem and London, 1932–50)
TSGT	*Transactions of the Society of Glass Technology* (Sheffield, 1916 f.)

Auth, *Newark*: S. H. Auth, *Ancient Glass at the Newark Museum* (Newark, 1976).

Brooks: J. A. Brooks, *Glass* (Maidenhead, 1975).

Brunton, *Qau*, III: G. B. Brunton, *Qau and Badari*, III (London, 1930).

Buckley, *OEG*: F. Buckley, *A History of Old English Glass* (London, 1925).

Calvi, *Aquileia*: M. C. Calvi, *I Vetri Romani del Museo di Aquileia* (Associazione Nazionale per Aquileia, 1968).

Charleston, 'Cambridge': R. J. Charleston, 'Cambridge Connoisseur', *Conn.*, CXLV (June, 1960), pp. 32–7.

Cooney, *British Museum*: J. D. Cooney, *Catalogue of Egyptian Antiquities in the British Museum*, IV, *Glass* (London, 1976).

Doppelfeld, *Köln*: O. Doppelfeld, *Römisches und fränkisches Glas in Köln* (Cologne, 1966).

Eisen, *Glass*: G. A. Eisen, with F. Kouchakji, *Glass, its Origin, History, Chronology, Technic and Classification to the Sixteenth Century* (New York, 1927).

English Glass Cat.: V &A, *English Glass Exhibition, 1968* (London, 1968).

Fremersdorf, *Vatican*: F. Fremersdorf, *Catalogo del Museo Sacro Vaticano*, V, *Antikes, islamisches und mittelalterliches Glas* (Vatican, 1975).

Froehner, *Gréau*: W. Froehner, *Collection Julien Gréau, Verrerie Antique, Émaillerie et Poterie appartenant à M. John Pierpont Morgan* (Paris, 1903).

Harden, *Karanis*: D. B. Harden, *Roman Glass from Karanis* (Ann Arbor, 1936).

Harden et al., *Masterpieces*: D. B. Harden, K. S. Painter, R. H. Pinder-Wilson and H. Tait, *Masterpieces of Glass* (British Museum exhibition, London, 1968).

Hartshorne, *OEG*: A. Hartshorne, *Old English Glasses* (London, 1897).

Hayes, *Toronto*: J. W. Hayes, *Roman and Pre-Roman Glass in the Royal Ontario Museum, Toronto* (Toronto, 1975).

Haynes, *Glass*: E. B. Haynes, *Glass through the Ages* (London, 1959).

Hollingworth and O'Reilly, *Girton*: E. J. Hollingworth and M. M. O'Reilly, *Anglo-Saxon Cemetery at Girton College, Cambridge* (Cambridge, 1925).

Honey, *Glass*: W. B. Honey, *Victoria and Albert Museum. Glass: a Handbook for the Study of Glass Vessels of All Periods and Countries* (London, 1946).

Isings, *Dated Finds*: C. Isings, *Roman Glass from Dated Finds* (Groningen, 1957).

Klesse, *Glas*: B. Klesse and G. Reineking-von Bock, *Glas* 2nd ed. (Cologne, Kunstgewerbemuseum, 1973).

La Baume and Salomonson, *Löffler*: P. La Baume and J. W. Salomonson, *Sammlung Karl Löffler* (Cologne, 1976).

Platz-Horster, *Berlin*: G. Platz-Horster, *Antike Gläser, Antikenmuseum, Berlin, Ausstellung 1976–7* (Berlin, 1976).

de Ridder, *de Clercq*: A. de Ridder, *Collection de Clercq*, VI, *Les Terres Cuites et les Verres* (Paris, 1909).

von Saldern et al., *Oppenländer*: A. von Saldern, B. Nolte, P. La Baume and T. E. Haevernick, *Gläser der Antike, Sammlung Erwin Oppenländer* (Mainz, 1974).

Smith Coll.: *Glass from the Ancient World, the Ray Winfield Smith Collection* (exhibition, Corning Museum of Glass, New York, 1957).

Spartz, *Kassel*: E. Spartz, *Antike Gläser, Staatliche Kunstsammlungen, Kassel* (Kassel, 1967).

Thomas, *Bomford*: (N. Thomas,) *Ancient Glass, the Bomford Collection of Pre-Roman and Roman Glass on loan to the City of Bristol Museum and Art Gallery* (Bristol, 1976).

Thorpe, *English and Irish*: W. A. Thorpe, *English and Irish Glass* (London, 1927).

Thorpe, *A History*: W. A. Thorpe, *A History of English and Irish Glass* (London, 1929).

MUSEUMS

BM   London, the British Museum
Mus. Arch. Ethn.: the Museum of Archaeology and Ethnology, Cambridge
RA   London, Royal Academy
V&A   London, Victoria and Albert Museum

LOAN EXHIBITS

From the Museum of Archaeology and Ethnology   **23a, 25b, 33, 45, 55, 57, 58b, 64–6, 68–73, 75–6, 78–81, 87–9, 91, 95, 98a, 102c, 104, 106, 113–18, 224**
    including items on extended loan:
    from the Mistress and Fellows of Girton College   **74, 86**
    from the former Huntingdonshire County Council   **67**
    from Colonel G. T. Hurrell   **77**
From Major R. Ades   **134**

100

PART I THE ANCIENT WORLD

MESOPOTAMIA

Glass vessels seem to have made their first appearance in the 16th and 15th centuries BC, mainly in Mesopotamia and its vicinity, although techniques for producing such soda-glass seem already to have been known then for several centuries, if little used, and those for inducing vitreous glazes on steatite and quartz fritware (or 'faience') had been practised for a much longer period. The early Mesopotamian vessels in question seem mostly to have been made around a clay core of the shape of the interior of the vase, which was rotated on a rod as glass was trailed over it to cover it, decoration being added by trailing on bands of contrasting colours which were drawn up and down into patterns and marvered into the surface. Sadly, this early Mesopotamian glass has survived the corrosive action of the soil only poorly.

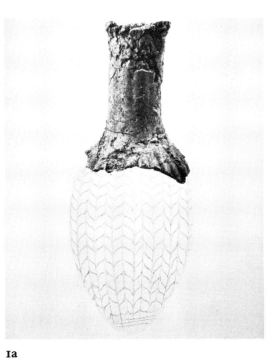

1a

1 FRAGMENTS OF PIRIFORM TOILET BOTTLES

Mesopotamian, c. 1400 BC or slightly later

From Tell al Rimah, Iraq. Given by the British School of Archaeology in Iraq.

a. Upper half of piriform bottle, from fill of c. 1350 BC over Old Babylonian palace. Core-formed; colours obliterated by surface corrosion, but ultra-violet examination confirms that neck is covered with trailed loop pattern and body with trailed 'feather' pattern. Preserved H: 10.4 cm. Estimated original H: 21 cm. E.3.1977.

b–g. Fragments from the rim (**b**), neck (**c**) and body (**d–g**) of similar bottles, from fill of c. 1250 BC. Core-formed; decoration in yellow and white on darker matrix whose colour is no longer securely identifiable. Preserved H: 1.5–3.5 cm. E.4–9.1977.

Cf. E. E. D. M. Oates in *Iraq* XXIX (1967), p. 93, pl. xxxviie, *Iraq* XXXII (1970), p. 3, pl. iii*b*, *e*; A. L. Oppenheim, R. H. Brill, D. Barag and A. von Saldern, *Glass and Glassmaking in Ancient Mesopotamia* (Corning, 1970), pp. 138, 143–5, 152–3, figs. 6–7, 19, 21, 38.

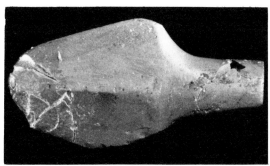

2

2 SPEARHEAD

Mesopotamian, perhaps of Achaemenid or Seleucid date, c. 6th–2nd centuries BC (?)

Opaque red. Probably moulded, but finished by grinding; tapering hole inside socket, formed in soft metal. Preserved H: 6.5 cm. E.47.1946.

No record of provenance. Bequeathed by O. C. Raphael.

Originally fastened to a shaft? Possibly from a parade weapon or serving as a religious symbol, such as that of the god, Marduk. But inscribed moulded votive glass axe-heads also occur in the late 14th century BC at Nippur: cf. J. P. Peters, *Nippur*, II (New York and London, 1898), pp. 134, 143, 373; Oppenheim *et al.*, *Glass in Mesopotamia*, pp. 148, 192, 215.

EGYPT

Fine glass vessels, jewellery and inlays appear in quantity in Egypt from the reign of Tuthmosis III (1490–1436 BC) with hardly any trace of an earlier period of experimentation. While the stimulus towards regular glass production may have been due to foreign contacts, the shapes and much of the decoration of the early vases are Egyptian, with prototypes in precious metals, stone or 'faience'. These vessels were core-formed (see above p. 11) the glass being applied to the core by trailing or dipping. Small objects were moulded, free-formed, or occasionally worked cold. Details were added by cutting, grinding and polishing. Beads were commonly formed by winding glass threads around a wire. Objects in glass are for unknown reasons rare after the 10th century BC, **19a** being a well-dated exception, until the art was revived in a new style in the 4th century BC.

NEW KINGDOM JEWELLERY AND INLAYS

3 FLY BEADS

Egyptian, mid 15th century BC

Gold *cloisonné* with translucent blue glass bodies and red jasper eyes. Each pair of flies L: 2.3 cm. E.67a.1939.

Given by G. D. Hornblower. Probably acquired with three rosette inlays (E.67.1939) from a wig cover similar to those found in the burial of three wives of King Tuthmosis III *c.* 1490–1436 BC; see H. E. Winlock, *The Treasure of Three Egyptian Princesses* (New York, 1948), pp. 14ff.

4 BEADS

Egyptian, 14th–13th centuries BC

a. Blue, yellow and brown. String L: 14.5 cm. E.6.1929.

From el-Amarna, from a house in the North Suburb. Gift of Egypt Exploration Society.

b. Blue and yellow rings with black and white 'eyes'. String L: 30.0 cm. E.176.1900.

From Abydos, Cemetery G. Gift of Egypt Exploration Fund.

c. Blue, yellow, turquoise and translucent yellow, strung in their original order. String L: 60.0 cm. E.51.1931.

3, 4b

From Matmar, grave 876, found on the neck of a child. Gift of the British Museum.

G. B. Brunton, *Matmar* (London, 1948), p. 59, pl. lxxiii.

5a, b

5 JEWELLERY

Egyptian, 14th–13th centuries BC

From Egypt. Given and bequeathed by G. D. Hornblower and R. G. Gayer-Anderson.

a. Earring, deep blue, with blue and white twisted trail. H: 2.8 cm. E.320.1939.

b. Ear-plugs, pink with blue and yellow trails, EGA.288.1947; translucent blue-green, EGA.286.1947; turquoise with yellow trail, E.322.1939; black with white and yellow trails, EGA.290.1947; pink with yellow trails, EGA.289.1947; black with red, white and yellow trails, EGA.324.1939. Average L: 3.0 cm.

c. Rings, translucent blue and brown incised with hieroglyphs meaning life and health. Bezels L: 1.8, 2.0 cm. EGA.131.1947, EGA.128.1947.

d. Ear-stud, yellow with twisted trails of turquoise and white. D: 2.7 cm. EGA.2505.1943.

Cf. Cooney, *British Museum*, for **a**: no. 999; for **b**: nos. 975–83, 986–98; for **c**: nos. 1035, 1037; for **d**: no. 1834.

6 INLAYS

Egyptian, moulded, *c.* 14th–13th centuries BC

a. Male head, red. H: 1.8 cm. EGA.3259.1943. From Egypt. Gift of R. G. Gayer-Anderson.

Cf. Cooney, *British Museum*, no. 940.

b. Vulture, white. H: 5.0 cm. E.62.1921.

From Kôm Medînet Ghurab, tomb 6. Gift of British School of Archaeology in Egypt.

G. B. Brunton and R. Engelbach, *Gurob* (London, 1927), p. 9, pl. xxix 19.

c. Snake head, deep blue. L: 2.2 cm. E.427.1954. From Egypt. Bequeathed by Sir Robert Greg.

Cf. J. Cooney in *JGS* II (1960), p. 18 fig. 8.

6b

TOILET VESSELS

7 FRAGMENTS OF VASES

Egyptian, core-formed, 1365–1345 BC

From el-Amarna, Petrie excavations 1891–2. Bequeathed by Sir Herbert Thompson.

a. Rim fragment of krateriskos with trailed 'feather' pattern of yellow, turquoise and white on purple. L: 2.5 cm. E.22.1944.

b. Rim fragment of krateriskos with trailed wavy line pattern of yellow and white on translucent blue. L: 3.2 cm. E.30e.1944.

c. Shoulder fragment of krateriskos with trailed wavy line and garland patterns and two impressed 'eyes' in yellow, turquoise and white on translucent blue. L: 3.8 cm. E.28e.1944. This is the only example of an Amarna vase with the 'eye' pattern (see B. Nolte, *Die Glasgefässe im Alten Ägypten* (Berlin, 1968), p. 24; D. Barag in A. L. Oppenheim, R. H. Brill, D. Barag and A. von Saldern, *Glass and Glassmaking in Ancient Meso-*

potamia (Corning, 1970), p. 184) whose shape can be reconstructed.

d. Fragment from lower body of a vase with trailed 'feather' pattern in yellow and turquoise on green. L: 4.0 cm. E.23.1944.

W. M. Flinders Petrie, *Tell el Amarna* (London, 1894), pp. 16, 27; cf. Nolte, *Glasgefässe*, for **a**: pl. xiv 26, for **b**: pl. xv 35; Cooney, *British Museum*, nos. 573–736, 1867.

8 EYE-PAINT JARS

Egyptian, core-formed, of palm-column shape with trailed 'feather' pattern decoration, 14th–13th centuries BC

a. Yellow and white on deep blue. H: 7 cm. E.112.1932.

Bequeathed by E. Towry Whyte.

M. A. Murray, *The Splendour that was Egypt* (London, 1949), p. 121, pl. lxxxvi 4; Nolte, *Glasgefässe*, p. 146 no. 30.

b. Opaque light blue-grey with yellow and white trails and four-pointed design under foot. H: 7.5 cm. E.200.1900.

Purchased in Egypt by Sir Flinders Petrie.

Nolte, *Glasgefässe*, p. 147 no. 47.

c. Deep blue with a corroded purplish surface, with white, yellow and pale green trails. H: 9 cm. E.201.1900.

Acquired with **b**.

Nolte, *Glasgefässe*, p. 146 no. 32.

9 EYE-PAINT JAR

Egyptian, core-formed, 1365–1345 BC

Palm-column shape, deep blue with trailed feather pattern in turquoise and white. H: 9.8 cm. E.1.1938.

From el-Amarna. Gift of Percy Newberry.

Murray, *Splendour*, p. 121, pl. lxxxvi 5; Nolte, *Glasgefässe*, p. 148 no. 42.

10 AMPHORISKOS

Egyptian, core-formed, *c.* 13th century BC

Wine-coloured with trailed 'feather' pattern in yellow, turquoise and white. H: 7.9 cm. E.69.1921. Similar vases have been found in Cyprus, Rhodes and the Levant, where they are presumably exports from Egypt.

8a, 9, 8b, 8c   7c

13 KING'S HEAD

Egyptian, moulded, Dynasty XXVI, 664–525 BC

Head of a king wearing the *nemes* headcloth with the uraeus serpent on his brow, deep blue imitating lapis lazuli. H: 3.8 cm. E.FG.3.

14 MAN'S HEAD

Egyptian, Ptolemaic period, 332–30 BC

Opaque turquoise, moulded then finished by cutting, and incision (of ears and eyes). H: 1.7 cm. EGA.181.1947.

From Egypt. Bequest of R. G. Gayer-Anderson.

10

From Kôm Medînet Ghurab, group 705F from Petrie's excavations in 1920. Gift of British School of Archaeology in Egypt.

Brunton and Englebach, *Gurob*, pl. liii; Nolte, *Glasgefässe*, pp. 112, 119 no. 39, pl. xix.

11 EYE-PAINT CYLINDER

Egyptian, core-formed, Ptolemaic period 332–30 BC

Opaque turquoise with bronze rings to hold the applicator stick. H: 5.0 cm. EGA.3230.1943.

From Egypt. Given by R. G. Gayer-Anderson.

SCULPTURE

12 FOOT

Egyptian, moulded, 1365–1345 BC

Opaque red with yellow veining, from a composite statuette of a man. L: 5.2 cm. E.30.1927.

From el-Amarna, from a house in the South Central Quarter. Gift of the Egypt Exploration Society.

H. Frankfort and J. D. S. Pendlebury, *The City of Akhenaten*, II (London, 1933), p. 15.

INLAYS OF ELEVENTH TO FIRST CENTURIES BC

Glass was used in inlays as a substitute for semi-precious stones such as turquoise, lapis lazuli and jasper. Geometric inlays were applied as pure decoration (see **15d**) but glass was also shaped into representations of human and animal figures, as well as objects and hieroglyphs. These decorated objects of all kinds, furniture, wall tiles, boxes, jewellery and statues, although inlays from shrines and coffins have survived in the largest quantities.

13, 14

15c, d

15 INLAYS

Egyptian, *c.* 11th–9th centuries BC, except for **a** which is probably Ptolemaic, 4th–1st centuries BC

a. Outline of left eye, translucent dark blue. From a mummy of a sacred bull or cow. H: 6.3 cm. E.117.1932.

Bequest of E. Towry Whyte.

Cf. Cooney, *British Museum*, no. 925; Sir Robert Mond and O. Myers, *The Bucheum* (London, 1934), pp. 65–7, pls. cxvii–cxxii.

b. Dark blue fragments of two moulded scarabs. From coffins. H: 4.0 cm, 7.0 cm. EGA. 1435.1943, EGA.1510.1943.

From Egypt. Gift of R. G. Gayer-Anderson.

c. Pair of eyes, outlined in dark blue glass. From coffins, masks or statues. L: 3.5 cm, 3.6 cm. EGA.247.1949.

From Egypt. Bequest of R. G. Gayer-Anderson.

d. Beard of gilded wood inlaid with blue glass. From a mummiform coffin. H: 16.5 cm. E.105. 1932.

From Karnak. Bequest of E. Towry Whyte.

Sotheby's Catalogue, 13 January 1891, lot 293.

16 INLAYS

Egyptian, mainly Ptolemaic, *c.* 4th–1st centuries BC

Moulded, except for **j** which are cut out from flat glass. Mainly from coffins, and small shrines. H: 1.4–5.3 cm.

Given or bequeathed by the Rev. G. J. Chester, R. G. Gayer-Anderson, G. D. Hornblower, Dr G. F. Rogers and E. Towry Whyte.

a. Column drums: red, EGA.3281.1943; bright blue, EGA.3900.1943. **b.** Obelisks: deep blue, EGA.240.1949; light blue-grey with white, deep blue and red inlay, E.115.1932. **c.** Lintel, deep blue, EGA.242.1949. **d.** Starry sky, bright blue, EGA. 245.1949. **e.** Feather crown, deep blue, EGA. 3273.1943. **f.** *Atef* crown of Osiris, deep red, E.168.1891. **g.** Crown of Lower Egypt, bright blue, EGA.243.1949. **h.** Wig, bright blue, EGA. 3273.1943. **i.** Male heads: red with white patina, E.186.1934; red with blue wig, E.613.1939; light blue, EGA.254.1949. **j.** Feather crowns: yellow,

EGA.1557.1943; black, E.67.1891; white, EGA. 3270.1943. **k.** Uraei: greenish blue, EGA.235. 1949; light blue, EGA.3263.1943. **l.** Head of an ibis, black with orange, red and white, EGA.234. 1949. **m.** Chest and arm of a man making offerings, bright red, EGA.3278.1943. **n.** Hieroglyphs: human face, bright red, E.581.1939; water sign, black, EGA.1776.1943; *djed* column, deep blue, E.559.1939. **o.** Torsos of Four Sons of Horus, deep blue (two), deep red, green, EGA.2192–5.1943. **p.** Lions, bright red, E.55.1940. **q.** Legs of seated and standing figures: turquoise, E.567.1939; deep red, EGA.3274.1943.

AMULETS

Whether worn during life or laid among the bandages of the mummy after death, amulets were indispensable to the well-being of the Egyptian. Divinities or their attributes were associated with particular areas of life, Bes with children, Tueris with child-bearing, or with particular virtues, Thoth with wisdom, Isis with love. Most amulets

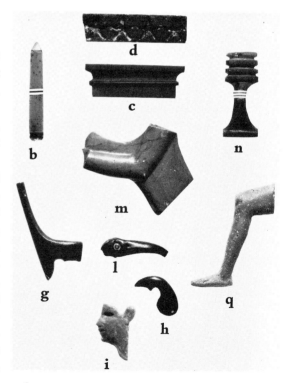

16

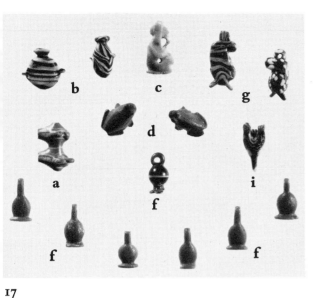

17

19a, 18

were however protective, ensuring the wearer's health, or happiness, and were called on above all at the critical moment of the passage through death to the next world.

17 AMULETS OF THE NEW KINGDOM

Egyptian, 14th–13th centuries BC. H: 1.0–2.6 cm

Given or bequeathed by R. G. Gayer-Anderson, E. Towry Whyte, Sir Robert Greg, the Rev. G. J. Chester, J. J. Stevenson and G. D. Hornblower.

a. Ducks, blue with yellow and white trails, E.327.1932, E.432.1954. **b.** Hearts: blue with white trails, E.326a.1932, E.74.1891; dark blue with yellow, white and turquoise trails, E.326d.1932. **c.** Royal child, turquoise blue, EGA.4640.1943. **d.** Frogs, red, E.487.1954, EGA.1681.1943. **e.** Lotus flower, turquoise, E.72.1891. **f.** Lotus seeds: deep blue with yellow trails, EGA.6220.1943; blue, E.10.a–f.1935. **g.** The goddess Tueris: brown with yellow trails, E.309.1939; deep blue with yellow and white trails, EGA.6233.1943; black spattered with white and red drops, E.324.1932. **h.** Crescent. blue, E.292.1947. **i.** Head of jackal, deep blue with white trails, E.319.1939.

18 AMULET OF KESY

Egyptian, c.13th century BC

'Girdle of Isis' meaning stability. Red, moulded, with incised inscription naming the deceased official, Kesy. H: 5.8 cm. E.47.1940.

Given by D. H. T. Hanbury.

19 ISIS AND HORUS

Egyptian, c. 9th–8th centuries BC

a. Isis suckling Horus, moulded, deep blue. H: 3.2 cm. E.215.1931.

From Matmar, from the intact grave of a woman. Gift of the British Museum.

G. B. Brunton, *Matmar* (London, 1948), pl. lviii 27; J. Cooney in *JGS* II (1960), p. 29.

b. Pendant plaque, incised with figure of Horus, translucent blue. H: 2.1 cm. EGA.6305.1943.

Such objects are also found in the late New Kingdom, from 13th century BC.

From Egypt. Gift of R. G. Gayer-Anderson.

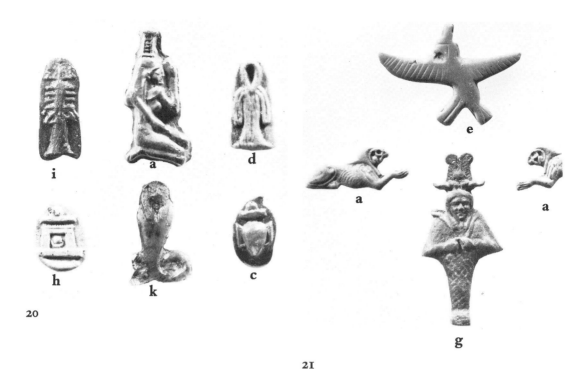

20

21

20 RELIEF AMULETS

Egyptian, moulded, Ptolemaic, 332–30 BC (except for **e** which could date from the 13th century BC) H: 2.8–5.7 cm.

Given or bequeathed by E. Towry Whyte, R. G. Gayer-Anderson, and Dr G. F. Rogers.

a. Mourning Nephthys, red, E.380.1932. **b.** Mourning woman, blue EGA.2230.1943. **c.** Heart, red, EGA.1927.1943. **d.** 'Girdle of Isis', turquoise, EGA.1917.1943. **e.** Scarab, translucent blue, E.254.1934. **f.** Thoth, translucent brown, turquoise, EGA.1918–19.1943. **g.** Plumb line, blue, EGA.1921.1943. **h.** Shrine with moon disc, yellow, E.113.1932. **i.** *Djed* pillar (backbone of Osiris), blue, EGA.2238.1943. **j.** Table of offerings, yellow, EGA.2205.1943. **k.** Lion-headed cobra, translucent blue, E.378.1932.

21 PTOLEMAIC AMULETS

Egyptian, *c.* 4th–1st centuries BC
All moulded, but **e** also shows incised detail.
Given or bequeathed by D. H. T. Hanbury, E. Towry Whyte, the Rev. G. S. Bird, R. G. Gayer-Anderson, and Sir Robert Greg.

a. Hawk-headed lions, turquoise and green, E.55.*a*–*b*.1940. **b.** Cattle bound for sacrifice: white, E.381.1932; orange, E.29.1934; dark and pale blue, yellow, E.385.1932. **c.** Sekhmet presenting *djed* column, yellow, brown, turquoise, E.379. 1932. **d.** Horus falcon, red, EGA.2077.1943. **e.** Soul bird, turquoise, E.A.48. **f.** 'Girdle of Isis', red, E.A.56. **g.** Osiris, red, E.370.1954. **h.** Bes, blue, EGA.1812.1943. **i.** Isis and Horus, dark blue, EGA.2000.1943.

22 AMULETS

Egyptian, moulded in translucent metal, late Ptolemaic–early Roman, *c.* 1st century BC–1st century AD

Given by R. G. Gayer-Anderson and G. D. Hornblower.

a. Horus the child: amber, EGA.5988.1943; clear, E.123.1939. **b.** Bes: green, EGA.2001.1943; clear, E.124.1939. **c.** Frog, green, EGA.1659.1943.

OTHER REGIONS UP TO THE ADVENT OF GLASS-BLOWING

GRAECO-PHOENICIAN CORE-GLASS

Although Egyptian manufacture of core-formed glass vessels appears to have halted in the 10th century BC, the technique was revived in Mesopotamia and may have been acquired thence by the Phoenicians. These unguent bottles are thought to have been produced in Phoenicia and probably also at various Greek centres. Their range of shapes is almost purely Greek and their wide distribution much the same as that of Greek pottery.

23 ARCHAIC AND CLASSICAL TOILET VESSELS

C. late 6th–5th centuries BC

Core-formed; deep blue, decorated in yellow and turquoise.

Given by M. F. Ransom and Sir William Elderton and bequeathed by F. McClean and L. B. Marlay.

a. Alabastron. H: 9.5 cm. Mus. Arch. Ethn. RC.23.727a.

Cf. Hayes, *Toronto*, pp. 8–9 no. 1, pl. i.

b. Amphoriskos. H: 7.7 cm. GR.21.1955.

Cf. Hayes, *Toronto*, p. 10 no. 9, pl. i.

c. Aryballos. H: 6.3 cm. GR.24c.1904.

Cf. Hayes, *Toronto*, p. 11 nos. 14–15, pl. i

d. Oinochoe. H: 11.0 cm. GR.2g.1912.

Cf. Auth, *Newark*, p. 40 no. 29.

24 TOILET VESSELS OF ARCHAIC OR CLASSICAL DATE

C. late 6th–5th centuries BC

Core-formed; white, decorated in deep mauve.

a. Alabastron. H: 11.8 cm. GR.40.1876.

From Karpassia, Cyprus. Formerly collection of A. P. di Cesnola.

23a, b, d, c

24b, 24a, 26a, 25a, 26b, 25b

Cf. P. Fossing, *Glass Vessels Before Glass-blowing* (Copenhagen, 1940), p. 60, fig. 29; Hayes, *Toronto*, p. 11 nos. 17–18, pl. i.

b. Oinochoe. H: 7.3 cm. E.51.1913.

From Deve Hüyük in Mesopotamia.

Cf. Fossing, *Vessels*, p. 74, fig. 50; Hayes, *Toronto*, pp. 11–12 no. 19, pl. ii.

25 TOILET VESSELS OF CLASSICAL DATE

C. 5th century BC

a. Amphoriskos. Core-formed; bright blue, decorated in yellow and turquoise. H: 8.1 cm. GR.GL.39.

Cf. Hayes, *Toronto*, p. 10 nos. 12–13, pl. i; Platz-Horster, *Berlin*, p. 13 no. 9.

b. Alabastron. Core-formed; deep amber, decorated in turquoise and yellow. H: 9.4 cm. Mus. Arch. Ethn. RC.23.727*b*.

From Cyprus (?). Ransom collection.

Cf. Hayes, *Toronto*, pp. 9–10 nos. 7–8, pl. i; A. von Saldern *et al.*, *Oppenländer*, pp. 57, 72, nos. 184–5.

26 LATE CLASSICAL OR EARLY HELLENISTIC TOILET VESSELS

C. 4th–3rd centuries BC

Bequeathed by Sir Robert Mond and C. B Marlay.

a. Alabastron. Core-formed; bright blue, decorated in white and yellow. H: 9.9 cm. E.55.1946.

Cf. Fossing, *Vessels*, p. 107, figs. 76–8; Hayes *Toronto*, p. 12 no. 20, pl. ii.

b. Oinochoe. Core-formed; deep bluish green with white bands and yellow trailing. H: 5.5 cm GR.2*h*.1912.

Cf. de Ridder, *de Clercq*, pp. 135–6 no. 240 pl. viii; Auth, *Newark*, p. 41 no. 30.

27 LATE HELLENISTIC TOILET VESSELS

C. 2nd–1st centuries BC

a. Alabastron. Core-formed; dark blue, decorated in yellow and white. H: 13.3 cm. GR.19. 1876.

27b, c, a

From Marion, Cyprus. Cesnola collection.
Cf. Fossing, *Vessels*, p. 111, fig. 83; Auth, *Newark*, p. 32 no. 14.

b. Amphoriskos. Core-formed; deep blue, decorated in yellow and white; amber handles. H: 11.0 cm. Mus.Arch.Ethn. RC.23.721*a*.

From Amathus, Cyprus. Ransom collection.
Cf. Hayes, *Toronto*, p. 15 no. 38; Auth, *Newark*, p. 38 no. 25.

c. Amphoriskos. Core-formed; deep blue, decorated in yellow and turquoise (partly turned white); clear handles. H: 15.1 cm. GR.84.1876.

From Marion, Cyprus. Cesnola collection.
Fossing, *Vessels*, p. 123, fig. 98.

28b, c, a

28 LATE AMPHORISKOI

C. 1st century BC – early 1st century AD

All from Cyprus; **b** and **c** from Amathus, formerly Cesnola collection.

a. Core-formed; black (?), decorated in yellow and white; amber handles and toe; fragmentary, showing inside the reddish core traces sometimes associated with Phoenician manufacture. H: 16.8 cm. GR.GL.74.

Cf. E. B. Dusenbery in *JGS* IX (1967), p. 37, fig. 7.

b. Core-formed; amber, decorated in yellow and white. H: 15.1 cm. GR.93.1876.

Cf. Hayes, *Toronto*, p. 15 no. 35, pl. iii; Auth, *Newark*, p. 39 nos. 26–7.

c. Core-formed; amber, decorated in yellow and turquoise (partly turned white); clear handles and toe. H: 14.9 cm. GR.104.1876.

Fossing, *Vessels*, p. 120, fig. 94.

29 HEAD-SHAPED BEADS AND PENDANTS

Phoenician, *c.* 6th–2nd centuries BC

Free-fashioned on a rod (or, in the case of **g**, partly moulded) in the colours of the vases **23–8** above: deep blue, white, yellow, mauve, turquoise and black. H: 1.7–4.8 cm.

Cesnola collection, R. G. Gayer-Anderson and G. D. Hornblower gifts and E. Towry Whyte bequest.

a. Head bead, decorated like the toilet vessels. E.351.1932.

b. Janiform head beads. EGA.4763.1943 (from Egypt), GR.106*c*.1876 (from Amathus, Cyprus).

c. Mask pendant. E.350*b*.1932.

d. Blue-bearded head pendant. GR.106.1876 (from Amathus).

e. Negroid (?) head pendant. GR.106*b*.1876 (from Amathus).

f. Satyr (?) head pendants. EGA.4764.1943 (from Egypt), E.350*a*.1932.

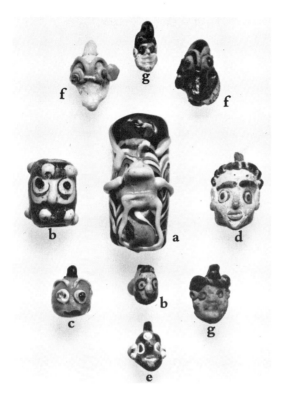

f   g   f

b   a   d

c   b   g

e

29

The technique used for these vessels in Syria, Greece and Italy seems also to have been first evolved in Mesopotamia. They appear to have been cast either by the *cire-perdue* method or in piece-moulds, and to have been finished by cutting and polishing on a wheel or lathe.

30 CONICAL OR MAMMIFORM BOWLS

Syrian, *c.* 2nd or early 1st century BC

From Cyprus. Cesnola collection.

a. From Amathus. Iridised amber metal; 5 engraved bands inside near lip; outside faintly abraded double and single concentric circles at foot (to take colour or gilding?). D: 14.0 cm. GR.1.1876.

b. From Salamis. Iridised clear bubbly metal; 3 pairs of engraved bands inside; outside apparently as **a**. D: 13.4 cm. GR.31.1876.

c. From Karpassia. Metal as **b**; triple engraved band inside below lip; outside apparently as **a**. D: 15.4 cm. GR.32.1876.

Cf. G. D. Weinberg in *JGS* XII (1970), pp. 17–27; Auth, *Newark*, p. 45 no. 33.

g. Garlanded head pendants. GR.106d.1876 (from Amathus), E.311.1939.

Cf. de Ridder, *de Clercq*, pp. 273–6, nos. 618–26, pl. xxxii; D. B. Harden in *Arch. J.* cxxv (1969), p. 57, pl. vi*e*.

30c, a, b

31 HEMISPHERICAL AND SIMILAR BOWLS

From Cyprus. Cesnola collection.

a. Syrian, *c.* 2nd or 1st century BC (and later?)

From Amathus. Iridised bubbly mauve metal; engraved band inside. D: 12.8 cm. GR.2.1876.

b. Syrian, *c.* 1st century BC

From Amathus. Iridised clear metal; double engraved bands inside below lip and outside at foot. D: 14.9 cm. GR.117.1876.

c. Syrian, *c.* late 1st century BC or early 1st century AD

From Marion. Iridised clear metal; single and double engraved bands inside. D: 11.3 cm. GR.30.1876.

Cf. Weinberg, *loc. cit.*; Hayes, *Toronto*, p. 18 nos. 40–2, pls. iii–iv.

31a, b, c

32 RIBBED BOWLS

a. Syrian, *c.* late 1st century BC or early 1st century AD

Iridised amber metal; 54 ribs at shoulder; engraved band inside below lip. D: 13.5 cm. GR.56.1876.

From Tremithus, Cyprus. Cesnola collection.

b. Syrian, *c.* mid 1st century AD

Iridised clear metal with greenish-blue tint; 34 moulded ribs radiating from base; 2 engraved bands inside. D: 15.1 cm. GR.38.1876.

From Idalion, Cyprus. Cesnola collection.

c. Probably Italian, *c.* mid 1st century AD, copying an earlier Syrian form.

Iridised clear metal with greenish tint; 97 moulded ribs at shoulder; inside, engraved band at lip; double, single and double engraved concentric circles on floor. D: 17.3 cm. GR.11.1943.

Given by Mrs S. Goetze.

Cf. Isings, *Dated Finds*, pp. 17–21, Forms 3*a*, *c*, *d*; Hayes, *Toronto*, pp. 19–20 nos. 47, 49, 50, fig. 2, pl. iv; also for **c**, Mus. Arch.Ethn. RC.23.731, from southern France.

33 FOOTED BEAKER

Egyptian (?), *c.* late 1st century AD

Almost colourless metal with faintest greenish-yellow tint; relief bands outside just under rim, below bottom of lip and at lower angle of body. H: 6.6 cm. Mus. Arch. Ethn. 48.1759.

From Panticapaeum in the Crimea, 'found in a street of tumuli leading towards Myrmecium'. Braybrooke collection.

An unusual cup shape, partly matched in decorated glass, e.g. R. E. M. and T. V. Wheeler in *Archaeologia* LXXVIII (1928), p. 170 no. 1, pl. xxxiv 1,

32a, b, c

no. I. Possibly related to the blown so-called stem-less '*carchesium*', which appears at about the same time; cf. Isings, *Dated Finds*, pp. 50–2, Form 36*b*.

33

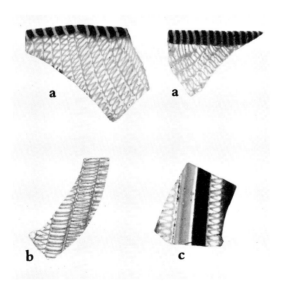

34

This luxury decoration was achieved by elaborate trailing (as in the 'agate' glass) or by constructing the vessel from coloured rods, sometimes themselves built up into layered patterns (as in the *mille-fiori* glass) or translucent with spiral trailing (as in the lace or *reticella* glass). These techniques apparently reached their height in the Hellenistic kingdoms, especially Egypt and Syria, and spread to Italy, where they flourished at the beginning of our era. The vases themselves were still core-formed or moulded.

34 FRAGMENTS OF MOULDED LACE-GLASS BOWLS

Alexandrian (?), *c.* 3rd century BC – early 1st century AD

From Egypt (?). Bequeathed by E. Towry Whyte.

a. Made from colourless rods with white trailing; blue and white rim. Preserved H: 2.9, 1.9 cm. E.434*a*4.1932, E.434*a*10.1932.

b. Colourless rods with yellow trailing. Maximum dimension 3.5 cm. E.434*a*54.1932.

c. Colourless rods with white twist combined with plain green, yellow, blue and colourless rods, Maximum dimension 2.6 cm. E.434*a*36.1932.

Cf. D. B. Harden and A. Oliver in *JGS* x (1968), pp. 21–47 figs. 18–19, pp. 48–70 figs. 3, 9–10, 15; *JGS* XVII (1975), pp. 41–2 figs. 14–15.

35 FRAGMENTS OF MOULDED *MILLEFIORI* BOWLS

Alexandrian (?), *c.* 1st century BC (**a**) – 1st century AD (**b–e**).

From Egypt (?). Given by Dr G. F. Rogers and bequeathed by E. Towry Whyte.

a. Rim. Translucent pale mauve, blue, amber and white. Preserved W: 4.7 cm. E.434*a*2.1932.

36, 37, 38

b. Rim. Blue with white, red and yellow flowers and yellow and green flowers. Preserved H: 2.7 cm. E.187c.1934.

c. Rim. Red panels with yellow and green flowers bordered by mauve laced with green and yellow. Preserved H: 3.6 cm. E.187e.1934.

d. Floor, with engraved concentric circles. Mauve with white blobs and yellow and green flowers with red centres. Longest dimension: 3.6 cm. E.187g.1934.

e. Rim. Green, with yellow, red and white. Preserved H: 3.9 cm. E.187f.1934.

36 GOLD-BAND TOILET BOTTLE

Alexandrian (?), early or mid 1st century AD

Core-formed; green, blue, white, yellow and colourless bands, the latter encasing gold leaf. H: 8.8 cm. GR.20.1917.

Given by C. F. Murray; ex-coll. Forman.

Cf. Isings, *Dated Finds*, pp. 23–4, under blown Form 7; A. Oliver in *JGS* IX (1967), p. 23, especially figs. 14–15; von Saldern *et al.*, *Oppenländer*, pp. 104, 106, no. 274. This piece: Brooks, p. 4.

37 *MILLEFIORI BOWL*

Syrian (?), first half of the 1st century AD

Moulded, with mauve ring foot coiled on afterwards; honeycomb-like pattern made up of roughly hexagonal sections of mauve, red and white rod. D: 9.2 cm. GR.1.1973.

Given by the Friends of the Fitzwilliam; ex-coll. Kelekian.

Catalogue, Charles Ede Ltd., Roman Glass (London, April 1973), no. 20; *Annual Report of Fitzwilliam Museum Syndicate*, 1973, pp. 9, 23, pl. ii.

Cf. Isings, *Dated Finds*, p. 17, Form 2; Hayes, *Toronto*, pp. 24–5 nos. 59–63, fig. 2, pl. v; Auth, *Newark*, p. 55 nos. 47–8.

38 'AGATE'-GLASS TOILET BOTTLE

Italian (?), early or mid 1st century AD

Core-formed; brown and white marbling. H: 7.3 cm. GR.21.1917.

Given by C. F. Murray; ex-coll. Forman.

Cf. Isings, *Dated Finds*, pp. 22–3, under blown Form 6; Calvi, *Aquileia*, pp. 36, 48 no. 88, pl. v 2; Auth, *Newark*, p. 196 no. 311.

39 a, c, b, d

39 BEADS, ETC., WITH COLOURED DECORATION

Including gifts from British School of Archaeology in Egypt, R. G. Gayer-Anderson and Dr G. F. Rogers.

a. 'Eye-beads' from the Argive Heraeum, Greece; *c.* 8th–6th centuries BC

Black with marvered yellow and white trailing. Longest dimension: 2.0 cm. GR.44–5.1970.

Archaeological Reports 1970–1, pp. 69–70 no. *2r*, fig. 2.

b. 'Eye-beads' from Cemetery 700, Qâw el-Kebîr, Egypt; *c.* 6th–2nd centuries BC.

White, deep blue and amber 'eyes' in turquoise matrix. L. of string (including coral and fritware): 18.3 cm. E.36.1923.

Brunton, *Qau*, III, pl. xliii 19.

c. *Millefiori* button from Egypt; *c.* 1st–2nd centuries AD.

Green and yellow. D: 2.9 cm. E.187*h*.1934.

d. Assorted *millefiori* and other beads from Egypt; the majority probably *c.* 1st century BC – 4th century AD.

As strung, L: 31 cm. EGA.6332.1943.

40 GAMES AND GAMESMEN FROM GRAECO-ROMAN EGYPT

Egyptian, the majority probably *c.* 1st century BC – 2nd century AD

Given by R. G. Gayer-Anderson, G. D. Hornblower and Dr G. F. Rogers.

a. Dice. Blue with drilled markings (H: 1.55 cm), E.291.1939. Grey inlaid with white and deep blue (H: 1.45 cm), EGA.2492.1943.

b. Conical gamesmen. Multicoloured banded metal. H: 1.2–2.6 cm. EGA.2384.1943, EGA.2386. 1943, EGA.2392–3.1943, EGA.2398.1943, EGA. 2440.1943.

c. Counters or gaming pieces. Green and yellow *millefiori* glass (cf. **39c**). D: 1.55–2.5 cm. E. 187*i*.1934, E.313.1939, EGA.2387.1943.

d. Balls or gaming counters. Veined in contrasting colours. D: 1.6–2.2 cm. EGA.2370–1.1943, EGA.2373–4.1943, EGA.2378.1943.

e. Knucklebone. Colourless; from two-piece mould. L: 1.55 cm. E.122.1939.

MOSAIC GLASS

Essentially this employs a much more elaborate form of the procedure adopted with *millefiori* glass, achieving figured representations or complex patterns by assembling countless rods of coloured glass. Originally developed in Mesopotamia in the second and first millennia BC, it had been adopted by the Egyptians by the fourth century BC and seems to have achieved its highest development in Egypt in Ptolemaic and early Roman times. The minute detail of some of the examples seems to have been attained by assembling the image as a core, stretching it to reduce its size and then slicing it up for use.

41, 42, 43, 44c

42 *Reverse, enlarged*

41 INLAY: GARDEN POOL HIEROGLYPH

Egyptian *c.* 3rd–2nd centuries BC

White zig-zags laid on to blue matrix. H: 0.95 cm. E.4a.1886.

From the decoration of a shrine at Gumaiyima, near Tanis, Egypt. Given by the Egypt Exploration Society.

Cf. W. M. F. Petrie *et al.*, *Nebesheh and Defenneh* (London, 1888), pp. 42–4, pl. xviii; Cooney, *British Museum*, p. 113 no. 1166.

42 INLAY: NEW COMEDY MASK (GARLANDED COURTESAN?)

Alexandrian, *c.* 1st century BC (?)

Other half of head presumably provided by second, reversed, slice from same core. Blue ground; white flesh, head-band; black eye details; red lips; red and mauve hair; yellow, red and black ivy garland. H: 2.9 cm. E.618.1939.

From Egypt (?). Given by G. D. Hornblower.

Cf. H. W. Müller, *Ägyptische Kunstwerke, Klein-funde und Glas in der Sammlung E. und M. Kofler-*

Truniger, Luzern (Berlin, 1964), pp. 154–6, especially nos. A222a–d, colour pl. viii; von Saldern *et al.*, *Oppenländer*, pp. 121, 126 nos. 335a–b.

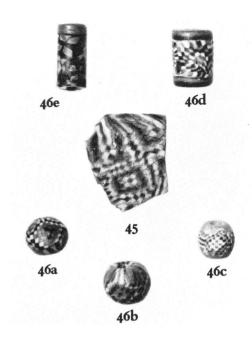

46e   46d

45

46a   46c

46b

43 PLATE FRAGMENT: FISH

Alexandrian, *c.* 1st century BC

 Light blue vessel; fish mosaic with mauve outline, scales green above, white below, with yellow and mauve modelling; fins mauve, yellow, red and green; eye, red, green, deep blue, yellow and white. Longest dimension: 4.8 cm. E.564.1939.

 From Egypt (?). Given by G. D. Hornblower.

 Cf. G. D. Weinberg in *JGS* IV (1962), pp. 29–36, especially figs. 4, 6 (seems more evolved than Athens bowl, assigned to 2nd century BC); Müller, *Kofler-Truniger*, pp. 163–6 nos. A235a–l, colour pl. xii; Fremersdorf, *Vatican*, pp. 45–6 nos. 282–6, pl. x and colour pl.

44 FRAGMENTS OF INLAY TILES

Egyptian, *c.* 1st century AD

 a–c floral with translucent blue ground and decoration in red, green, white, yellow and turquoise; d marbling in blended green, white and red.

 a. Longest dimension of largest fragment: 3.7 cm. E.34a–c.1904. From Oxyrhynchus. Given by the Egypt Exploration Society.

 b. Longest dimension of larger fragment: 5.6 cm. E.187a–b.1934. From Egypt. Given by Dr G. F. Rogers.

 c. Longest dimension: 5.35 cm. E.570.1939. From Egypt. Given by G. D. Hornblower.

 d. Dimensions: 6.0 × 3.7 cm. E.434a11.1932. From Egypt (?). Bequeathed by E. Towry Whyte.

 For a–c cf. Müller, *Kofler-Truniger*, p. 162 nos. A234a–x, colour pls. x–xi (likewise from Oxyrhynchus, as also V & A 1303–1904, 694–1905);

Cooney, *British Museum*, pp. 132–4 nos. 1642–63. For **d** cf. Fremersdorf, *Vatican*, pp. 41–3 nos. 211–56, pls. viii–ix.

45 RIM FRAGMENT FROM BOWL

Egyptian (or Italian?), *c.* 1st century AD

 Moulded; mosaic checkerboard pattern of square rods of mauve, red, white, yellow and turquoise. Preserved H: 2.4 cm. Mus. Arch. Ethn. AR.1902.306.

 From Lakenheath Warren, Suffolk.

 Cf. *Smith Coll.*, p. 82 no. 132; Cooney, *British Museum*, p. 139 no. 1713, colour pl. ii.

46 MOSAIC-GLASS BEADS

Egyptian, *c.* 1st century AD or slightly later

 From Egypt. Given by R. G. Gayer-Anderson.

 a–c. Spherical beads assembled from similar checkerboard rods and in the same colours as **45**. D: 1.0–1.7 cm. EGA.6330a–c.1943.

d. Similar cylindrical bead, assembled flat in translucent blue matrix and rolled into shape. L: 1.4 cm. EGA.6330*d*.1943.

e. Cylindrical floral bead; yellow flowers on light blue ground; red and white flowers on deep blue ground; red end. Preserved L: 1.65 cm. EGA.6330*e*.1943.

For **a–c** cf. Brunton, *Qau*, III, pl. xlvi 175; for **e**, *ibid.*, pl. xlv 35.

43 *Enlarged*

Seals of glass were extensively produced in antiquity, apparently mostly moulded from impressions taken from examples in semi-precious stone, whose form and colour they also sought to reproduce, so that those described here copy crystal, green jasper, agate (sometimes rather garishly), nicolo, sapphire, cornelian, lapis lazuli and peridot. They include major masterpieces of ancient glyptic. The illustrations show impressions taken from the seals.

47 PHOENICIAN SEALS

C. 7th–6th centuries BC

a. Scaraboid: Egyptianizing Horus falcon. Colourless. L: 1.85 cm. E.30.1909.

From Cyprus. Given by Dr M. R. James.

b. Scarab: Hellinizing winged deity with snakes. Green. L: 1.5 cm. E.33.1975.

Bought from Hitchcock Fund. From Duke of Northumberland's collection.

48 CLASSICAL GREEK SEALS

5th century BC

W. M. Leake collection and given by Miss B. K. Burn.

a. Scaraboid: cow with calf. Clear, pitted. L: 3.2 cm. B.50 (CM).

J. H. Middleton, *The Engraved Gems of Classical Times, with a Catalogue of the Gems in the Fitzwilliam Museum* (Cambridge, 1891), p. vi no. 8.

b. Scaraboid: seated Penelope; inscribed:

ΓΗΝΗΛΟ Γ[Η.

Colourless. L: 1.95 cm. CM.83.1972.

Cf. G. Horster, *Statuen auf Gemmen* (Bonn, 1970), pp. 8–12, pl. i.

c. Scaraboid: man's head. Clear. L: 3.0 cm. B.49 (CM).

G. M. A. Richter, *Engraved Gems of the Greeks and the Etruscans* (London, 1968), pp. 97–8 no. 327, where earlier bibliography.

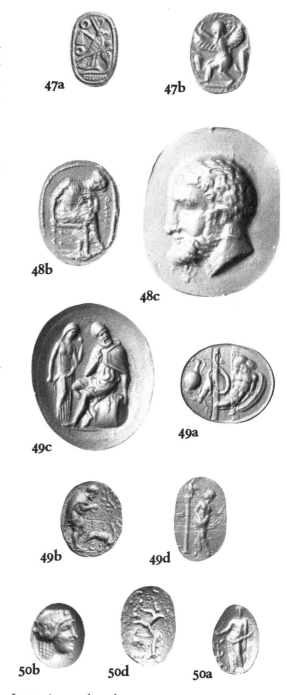

Impressions, enlarged

49 ITALIAN SEALS OF REPUBLICAN ROMAN DATE

C. 4th–1st centuries BC

Given by W. H. Caulfield and bequeathed by C. S. Ricketts and C. H. Shannon. All from rings.

a. Cadmus and snake. Remounted in modern ring; green, banded blue and white. L: 2.1 cm. S.15(CM).

Richter, *Greeks and Etruscans*, p. 204, no. 831.

b. Faustulus finding wolf with Romulus and Remus. Black, banded white. L: 1.85 cm. B.95 (CM).

Cf. G. M. A. Richter, *Engraved Gems of the Romans* (London, 1971), p. 21 no. 38.

c. Odysseus and Penelope. In its original gold ring; light blue laid over dark blue. L: 2.3 cm. S.16(CM).

C. H. Smith and C. A. Hutton, *Catalogue of the Antiquities in the Collection of the late Wyndham Francis Cook, Esqre.*, II (London, 1908), p. 38 no. 163, pl. vii.

d. Venus and dove. Green, banded blue and white. L: 1.5 cm. B.84(CM).

50 EARLY IMPERIAL ROMAN SEALS

C. 1st century BC–1st century AD

Given by W. H. Caulfield and Mrs Venn. All from rings.

a. Beardless Aesculapius. Translucent greenish blue. L: 1.3 cm. B.133(CM).

b. Garlanded theatrical mask. Deep amber. L: 1.9 cm. B.287(CM).

c. Priapus. Bright blue. L: 1.85 cm. B.179(CM).

d. Eagle, eaglet in tree. Green, L: 1.9 cm. B.202(CM).

EARLY SYRIAN BLOWN GLASS

There is little reliable testimony in ancient writings on the greatest of all innovations in glass-working, the invention of glass-blowing. It had presumably occurred by some date in the first century BC, since, from early in the first century AD, blown glass vessels occur in dated finds in steadily increasing numbers, at first overlapping with the later examples of the core-formed and moulded wares already considered. The most striking of all early blown glasses are the richly ornamented mould-blown vessels associated with Syria and, in particular, with the craftsmen of Sidon. These doubtless owed much to Syrian skills in glass-moulding and, on the as yet rather inadequate evidence from dated finds, may not have come into prominence much before the mid first century AD. Some of the early free-blown vessels still copy the colour effects of the old moulded and core-formed glass.

51

MOULD-BLOWN

51 INSCRIBED BEAKER

Syrian, *c.* mid (?) 1st century AD

Clear, with faint greenish tint, iridised; 3-piece mould (2 for sides, 1 for base); low ring foot;

52a, b

vertical fronds, horizontal bands and garlands; inscribed 'rejoice and be merry':

KATA(Ι)ΧΑΙΡΕ ΚΑΙ ΕΥΦΡΑΙΝΟΥ.

H: 7.7 cm. GR.60.1876.

From Marion, Cyprus. Cesnola collection.

D. B. Harden in *Syria* XXIV (1944–5), p. 91. Cf. Harden in *JRS* XXV (1935), pp. 171–3, pls. XXV*a–c*, xxvii*a*, xxviii 10–11.

52 TWO JARS

Syrian, *c*. mid (?) 1st century AD

a. Clear, with faint bluish tint, iridised; 2-piece mould; tongue pattern, leaf-scroll frieze, tongue pattern. H: 8.6 cm. GR.33*a*.1876.

From Tremithus, Cyprus. Cesnola collection. Acquired with painted lid, **98b**.

For decoration, cf. flask in Zara Museum assigned to Aristeas: M. C. Calvi in *JGS* VII (1965), p. 14 fig. 10; cf. also the amphoriskoi: N. B. Arakelian, G. A. Tiratzian and G. D. Khachatrian, *Glass of Ancient Armenia* (Yerevan, 1969), pp. 55–6, nos. 107–11; Auth, *Newark*, p. 70 no. 66.

b. Clear, with faint greenish tint, iridised; 3-piece mould (2 for walls, 1 for lower part); concentric circles under foot, acanthus *kymation*, tongue pattern, lattice frieze and Lesbian *kymation*. H: 8.8 cm. GR.118*a*.1876.

From Idalion, Cyprus. Cesnola collection. Also acquired with later lid (GR.118*b*.1876).

For lattice and tongues cf. von Saldern *et al.*,

Oppenländer, p. 160 no. 448; also jars signed by Ennion: e.g. *JGS* IV (1962), p. 50 no. 1, fig. 2; *JGS* X (1968), p. 181 no. 6.

53 TALL BEAKER

Syrian, *c*. mid (?) 1st century AD

Pale amber, iridised; 3-piece mould (2 for walls, 1 for base); concentric circles under foot; on sides plant-scrolls with trefoil leaves and tulip-like flowers (as on the tiles, **44**). H: 13.4 cm. GR.99. 1876.

From Soloi, Cyprus. Cesnola collection.

Cf. Thomas, *Bomford*, p. 18 no. 39.

Illustrated on p. 44

54 TWO TOILET BOTTLES

Syrian, *c*. mid (?) 1st century AD

a. Opaque white, iridised; 3-piece mould; following vessels shown in arcaded colonnade with grapes and garlands below: hydria, calyx-krater, olpe, hydria (or stamnos), oinochoe, fruit-filled kantharos; rim folded in. H: 7.7 cm. GR.23.1876.

From Cyprus. Cesnola collection.

b. Transparent light blue: 3-piece mould; resembles **a**, but larger and less detailed; vessels in arcaded colonnade: oinochoe, fruit-filled kantharos, olpe (?), oinochoe, fruit-filled calyx-krater, hydria; below, instead of garlands, pattern of overlapping lotus (?) petals; rim folded in and fire-rounded. H: 9.4 cm. GR.27.1876.

56, 55

From Larnaka, Cyprus. Cesnola collection.
Cf. Eisen, *Glass*, I, pp. 233–47; von Saldern *et al.*,
Oppenländer, pp. 142, 153, nos. 401–6.
Illustrated on p. 44

57

55 RIBBED BOWL

Syrian, mid or late 1st century AD

Clear with faint greenish tint; 3-piece mould (2 for sides, 1 for base); 107 ribs at shoulders; centre dot and 7 concentric circles on lower part. D: 13.2 cm. Mus. Arch. Ethn. RC.23.725.

From Cyprus(?). Ransom collection.

The blown equivalent of **32c**; cf. also **60a, b** below.

Calvi, *Aquileia*, p. 101. Cf. Hayes, *Toronto*, pp. 47–8 no. 82, fig. 2, pl. iv; Auth, *Newark*, p. 48 no. 39.

56 TALL BEAKER

Syrian, second half of 1st century AD

Pale amber; 3-piece mould; raised centre dot and 2 concentric circles under foot; on body 5 rows of almond-shaped and smaller hemispherical projections. H: 11.0 cm. GR.98.1876.

From Golgoi, Cyprus. Cesnola collection.

Cf. Isings, *Dated Finds*, pp. 45–6, Form 31; La Baume and Salomonson, *Löffler*, pp. 36–7 nos. 66, 68, colour pl. iv; Auth, *Newark*, p. 76 no. 79.

57 AMPHORISKOS

Syrian, *c*. late 1st century AD (?)

Transparent pale blue, with deep blue handles with turquoise veining; ill-matched 2-piece mould: moulded toe and 20 horizontal ribs; rounded rim, H: 8.1 cm. Mus. Arch. Ethn. RC.23.793.

From Cyprus (?). Ransom collection.

Calvi, *Aquileia*, p. 100. Cf. von Saldern *et al.*. *Oppenländer*, pp. 146–7, 156, nos. 420, 421, 423; also the one-handled version, *ibid.*, no. 422 and the taller amphoriskoi, *ibid.*, nos. 418, 422.

FREE-BLOWN

58 BLOWN TOILET BOTTLES COPYING CORE-FORMED COLOURED WARES

Syrian, early or mid 1st century AD

a. Iridised mauve with fine white trailing drawn up into loops; rim rolled inwards. H: 10.0 cm. GR.64.1876.

From Golgoi, Cyprus. Cesnola collection.

Cf. Thomas, *Bomford*, p. 20 no. 52; for dating, E. B. Dusenbery in *JGS* IX (1967), p. 41 nos. 16–17.

58b, 59, 58c, 58a

b. Deep blue with white (and light blue) looped up trailing; lip restored in gold in modern times. Restored H: 13.4 cm. Mus. Arch. Ethn. RC.23.728

From Cyprus (?). Ransom collection.

Cf. Isings, *Dated Finds*, pp. 34–5, Form 16; Hayes, *Toronto*, p. 51 no. 101, pl. ix.

c. Heavily iridised mauve with white trailing; 11 nipped ribs; lip missing. Preserved H: 8.7 cm. GR.10.1876.

From Karpassia, Cyprus. Cesnola collection.

Cf. Isings, *Dated Finds*, p. 41, Form 26*b*; Hayes, *Toronto*, p. 52 no. 109, pl. ix.

59 FLASK

Syrian, *c.* early to mid 1st century AD
Mauve; lip folded in and flattened. H: 16.8 cm. GR.6.1876.

From Amathus, Cyprus. Cesnola collection.

Cf. Isings, *Dated Finds*, pp. 34–5, Form 16; *QDAP* XII (1945), pp. 58–62, pl. xx 15.

60 RIBBED BOWLS

Syrian, *c.* mid 1st century AD
a. Clear with faint greenish-blue tint, iridised; 11 nipped ribs, rounded rim. D: 9.8 cm. GR.9.1876.

From Larnaka, Cyprus. Cesnola collection.

b. Translucent blue metal; 14 nipped ribs; incised lines outside at bottom of lip; rounded rim. D: 10.7 cm. GR.68.1876.

From Tremithus, Cyprus. Cesnola collection.

Cf., in other techniques, **32** and **55** above. Cf. Isings, *Dated Finds*, pp. 35–6, Form 17 (possibly slightly earlier in east(?); cf. E. B. Dusenbery in *JGS* IX, 1967, pp. 44–5); von Saldern *et al.*, *Oppenländer*, p. 101 no. 264.

60a, b

61b, a, c

61 PIRIFORM TOILET BOTTLES

Syrian, c. mid to late 1st century AD (?)

a. Plain bottle. Blue, with faint white looped trailing; rim rolled inwards. H: 11.3 cm. GR.70. 1876.

From Salamis, Cyprus. Cesnola collection.

Cf. Hayes, *Toronto*, pp. 52–3, no. 110, pl. ix.

b. Two-handled bottle. Clear, with bluish tint, iridised; rim folded in. H: 9.7 cm. GR.18.1888.

From Paphos, Cyprus. Given by the Cyprus Exploration Fund.

Cf. C. W. Clairmont, *Excavations at Dura-Europos*, IV, Part V, *The Glass Vessels* (New Haven, 1963), p. 30 no. 123, pl. xx.

c. Handled and footed variety (approximating to Italian amphoriskos in shape). Clear, with bluish tint, iridised; 'cut-out' foot; rim folded in. H: 11.6 cm. GR.15.1888.

From Paphos. Given by the Cyprus Exploration Fund.

Cf. Isings, *Dated Finds*, pp. 32–4, Form 15; Thomas, *Bomford*, p. 23 no. 73; Auth, *Newark*, p. 60 no. 55.

62 BOWL

Syrian, second half of 1st century AD

Clear with faint greenish-blue tint, iridised; 'cut-out' foot; rounded rim. D: 12.2 cm. GR.101. 1876.

From Leukolla, Cyprus. Cesnola collection.

Cf. Isings, *Dated Finds*, p. 89, Form 69a; La Baume and Salomonson, *Löffler*, p. 30 no. 36, pl. v 1.

63 HANDLED FLASK

Syrian, c. second half of 1st century AD (?)

Translucent blue; concave base; three-ribbed handle; folded rim. H: 18.3 cm. GR.5.1876.

From Tremithus, Cyprus. Cesnola collection.

Local Syrian shape that falls between Isings, *Dated Finds*, pp. 31–2, Form 14 and *ibid.*, pp. 69–70, Form 52a; for underlying shape of flask, cf. **93c** below.

62, 63

ROME AND THE WESTERN PROVINCES

The invention of glass-blowing vastly increased the range and availability of glass vessels and created an ever-growing demand for them throughout the Roman Empire. In Italy itself the beginning of our era seems to have seen an influx of Alexandrian and Syrian craftsmen and the development of flourishing local industries that were at their height in the first century AD. Production also quickly spread to the western provinces. From Italy the ways divided, either along the Mediterranean and up the Rhône to Lyons or via Aquileia, Switzerland and the Rhine to Cologne, where glass was made throughout the Roman period, from the mid 1st century AD. By the 2nd century, centres in northern Gaul and elsewhere in the Rhineland were also flourishing. As earlier in Italy, the interchange of ideas between the east Mediterranean and northern Europe continued for some time, but the unsettled state of the later Empire restricted such contacts, so that local styles diverged more widely. All items are free-blown unless otherwise stated.

64a, b

64 EARLY TOILET BOTTLES

a. Italian, early to mid 1st century AD
Piriform. Translucent blue; lip rolled inwards. H: 5.75 cm. Mus. Arch. Ethn. RC.23.822.
From Trier. Ransom collection.
Cf. Isings, *Dated Finds*, pp. 22–3, 42, Forms 6 and 28*a*; Fremersdorf, *Vatican*, p. 43 nos. 257–9, pl. xiii.

b. Italian, third quarter of 1st century to AD 79
Test-tube-shaped. Clear with greenish tint; rounded lip. H: 13.6 cm. Mus. Arch. Ethn. 48.1758.
From Pompeii. Braybrooke collection.
Cf. Isings, *Dated Finds*, p. 41, Form 27; Fremersdorf, *Vatican*, p. 53 nos. 413–4, pls. xv, xvi.

65 EARLY VESSELS FROM CEMETERY AT LITLINGTON, CAMBS.

Italian or early Rhenish (?), *c.* third quarter of 1st century AD
Cambridge Antiquarian Society collection; ex-coll. Webb.

65a, b

a. Handled flagon. Clear, with bluish tint; 'cut-out', slightly concave foot; 21 ribs on body 'optic'-blown; handle with central rib and, at its base, moulded medallion of child's head surrounded by 15 dots; lip folded inwards. H: 19.2 cm. Mus. Arch. Ethn. CAS.1883.791.

A. J. Kempe in *Archaeologia* XXVI (1836), pp. 371, 375, pl. xxvi 7, 12; Sir Cyril Fox, *Archaeology of the Cambridge Region* (Cambridge, 1948), p. 216, pl. xxv 4. Cf. Isings, *Dated Finds*, pp. 30-1, 70, between Forms 13 and 52*b*; Morin-Jean, *La Verrerie en Gaule sous l'Empire Romain* (Paris, 1913), pp. 116-18, fig. 143; for identical medallions from Cologne: F. Fremersdorf, *Die Denkmäler des römischen Köln*, VI, *Römisches geformtes Glas* (Cologne, 1961), pp. 43, 51-2, pls. lxxiii, cii.

b. Bowl. Clear with greenish tint; applied ring foot; tubular rim rolled outwards. D: 7.0 cm. Mus. Arch. Ethn. CAS.1883.792.

Cf. Isings, *Dated Finds*, pp. 59-60, Form 44*a*; Hayes, *Toronto*, pp. 153-4 no. 639, fig. 21, pl. xl.

66a, b

66 VESSELS FROM SHEFFORD, BEDS.

Italian and northern, *c.* late 1st century AD

Cambridge Antiquarian Society collection; ex-coll. Inskip.

a. Oinochoe, Italian (?). Deep translucent blue; slightly concave 'cut-out' foot; 20 'optic'-blown ribs on body; strap handle with pinched rotelles; rounded lip. H: 20.7 cm. Mus.Arch.Ethn. CAS. 1883.765.1.

This much older Greek shape is revived in Italian metalwork of 1st century AD; cf. also Isings, *Dated Finds*, pp. 74-6, Form 56.

b. Ribbed jar, northern. Amber; 'cut-out' foot; 16 'optic'-blown ribs on body; rim folded out and down. H: 13.2 cm. Mus. Arch. Ethn. CAS.1883. 765.4.

Cf. Isings, *Dated Finds*, p. 88, Form 67*c*; Fremersdorf, *Denkmäler*, VI, p. 44, pls. lxxvi-lxxvii. Shape also continues through 2nd century.

Sir Henry Dryden, *Roman and Roman-British Remains at and near Shefford, Co. Beds.* (*CASP* X, Cambridge, 1845), p. 13, pl. i 1-2; Fox, *Archaeology of the Cambridge Region*, p. 216, pl. xxvi 2.

67c, b, a

67 VESSELS FROM A BURIAL AT HUNTINGDON

Rhenish (?), end of 1st and early 2nd centuries AD

Found in inhumation at Three Nuns Bridge with coin of Hadrian, bronze vessel and pottery. Mus. Arch. Ethn., on permanent loan from former Hunts. County Council since 1967.

a. Square bottle containing ashes. Clear with bluish-green tint; mould-blown; base-mark: cross within circle; ten-ribbed handle; rim folded in. H: 24.8 cm.

Cf. Isings, *Dated Finds*, pp. 66-7, Form 51*b*; D. Charlesworth in *JGS* VIII (1966), pp. 26-40, figs. 7, 12.

b. Handled flask or flagon. Clear with greenish tint; concave 'cut-out' base and 'cut-out' ridge around lower body; ribbed handle (partly missing) has 'tail' with 12 notches; rim folded inwards. H: 26.0 cm.

Cf. Isings, *Dated Finds*, pp. 73–4, Form 55*b*.

c. Hexagonal bottle. Clear with greenish tint; mould-blown; base mark: 2 concentric circles; handle with 16 ribs; rim folded inwards. H: 20.1 cm.

Cf. Fremersdorf, *Denkmäler*, VI, p. 48, pl. xciii.

68   SQUARE BOTTLE

Rhenish (?), late 1st or early 2nd century AD

Iridised bubbly clear metal with greenish-blue tint; mould-blown; base mark: square with cross in centre and small triangular shapes at corners; handle with 3 ribs; rim folded in and flattened. H: 20.5 cm. Mus. Arch. Ethn. Z.21226.

From Haslingfield, Cambs. Cambridge Antiquarian Society Collection (W. K. Foster, gift, 1887).

D. Charlesworth in *JGS* VIII (1966), p. 39 no. 70.

69   FUNNEL

Italian or Rhenish (?), 1st or 2nd century AD

Clear with bluish tint; rounded lip. H: 7.6 cm. Mus. Arch. Ethn. RC.23.1662.

Uncertain provenance. Ransom collection.

Cf. Isings, *Dated Finds*, p. 92, Form 74; Fremersdorf, *Denkmäler*, VI, p. 37 pl. xlix; Auth, *Newark*, p. 156 no. 209.

71, 70, 69, 68

70   BATH FLASK

Probably Italian or northern, second half of 1st or 2nd century AD

Clear, with bluish-green tint; 'dolphin' handles with 'tail' trailed back upwards; lip folded outwards then rolled inwards. H: 2.9 cm. Mus. Arch. Ethn. Z.21202.

Uncertain provenance. Cambridge Antiquarian Society Collection (J. Barratt gift, 1886).

The Roman descendant of the Greek aryballos; cf. **23c**. Cf. also Isings, *Dated Finds*, pp. 78–81, Form 61.

71   JAR

Gaulish, second half of 1st or 2nd century AD

Iridised clear metal with bluish tint; concave base; rim rolled and folded under, lip flattened. H. 19.2 cm. Mus. Arch. Ethn. Z.21165.

From vicinity of Arras or Amiens. Cambridge Antiquarian Society collection (J. Barratt gift, 1886).

Cf. Isings, *Dated Finds*, pp. 86–7, Form 67*a*; Thomas, *Bomford*, p. 22, no. 71.

72   TWO-HANDLED LIDDED JAR (CINERARY URN)

Italian or Gaulish, late 1st or 2nd century AD

Clear, with bluish-green tint; concave 'cut-out' base; M-shaped handles with 'tail' trailed back across top; rim folded inwards. 'Bottle-neck' type lid with top folded in and flattened. H: 36.7 cm with lid, 31.0 cm without. Mus. Arch. Ethn. Z.21210.

Uncertain provenance. Cambridge Antiquarian Society collection (J. Barratt gift, 1886).

Cf. Isings, *Dated Finds*, pp. 81–3, 85–6, Forms 63, 66*b*; Honey, *Glass*, p. 27, pl. vi*a*.

72

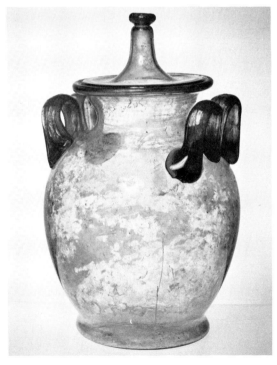

73

73 TWO-HANDLED LIDDED JAR (CINERARY URN)

Probably Gaulish, late 1st or 2nd century AD

Clear, with bluish tint; concave 'cut-out' base; M-shaped handles, with 'tail' trailed back across top; rim folded inwards. 'Bottle-neck' type lid with centre of top pushed in and 'cut-in' constriction below to separate knob. H: 39.3 cm with lid, 31.6 cm without. Mus. Arch. Ethn. Z.21164.

From vicinity of Arras or Amiens. Cambridge Antiquarian Society collection (J. Barratt gift, 1886).

As **72**, q.v., but more heavily proportioned and better executed.

74 BEAKER FROM GIRTON

Italian or Rhenish (?), c. mid (?) 2nd century AD

Colourless; 'pad' foot with edge ground smooth; 2 engraved bands on body; rim ground smooth. H: 9.4 cm.

Found in Roman grave II at Girton College with **86** and other glass and pottery. Mus. Arch. Ethn., on extended loan from Girton College since 1924.

An unusual shape, probably to be interpreted as a footed version evolved from Isings, *Dated Finds*, p. 45, Form 30.

Hollingworth and O'Reilly, *Girton*, pp. 32–4, pl. xi.

75 TWO-HANDLED OCTAGONAL BOTTLE

Rhenish (?), c. 2nd century AD

Iridised bubbly green metal; mould-blown; base mark: elongated octagon enclosing 3 circles, 2 outer of which each have 4 inscribed arcs forming a concave-sided lozenge; 3-ribbed handles; rim folded in and flattened. H: 26.0 cm. Mus. Arch. Ethn. 59.475.

From Glatton, Cambs. (formerly Hunts.). Bequeathed by Dr J. R. Garrood.

J. R. Garrood in *AJ* v (1925), pp. 287–9, figs. 1–2. Cf. Isings, *Dated Finds*, p. 108, Form 90.

74, 76, 75

76 HANDLED DOUBLE FLASK

Probably Gaulish, 2nd century AD

Clear, with bluish tint; flattened underneath; 3-ribbed handle; rims 'knocked off' and ground flat. H: 15.1 cm. Mus. Arch. Ethn. Z.21177.

From Arles. Cambridge Antiquarian Society collection (J. Barratt gift, 1886).

Cf. Morin-Jean, *Gaule*, p. 102, fig. 120; Auth, *Newark*, p. 103 no. 116; Thomas, *Bomford*, p. 25 no. 88.

77b, c, d

77 VESSELS FROM CEMETERY AT HAUXTON MILL, CAMBS.

Probably Rhenish, late 2nd or early 3rd century AD

Mus. Arch. Ethn., on permanent loan from Lt Col. G. T. Hurrell since 1956.

a. Flask. Colourless; 'pad' base with edge ground flat; on body fivefold pairs of ribs nipped together in middle and pinched out at bottom ends into exquisitely symmetrical pattern; cylindrical neck with constriction at base and horizontal trailing at top under out-splayed rounded lip. H: 22.8 cm.

b. Handled bottle-jug. Colourless; ring of shallow incisions on base; groups of 1, 2, 6, 2, 1 engraved bands on body; rim folded down and up. H: 20.1 cm.

c, d. Small bowls. Colourless; 'cut-out' ring feet; pontil marks on bases; round rims. D: 11.4 cm, 9.7 cm.

D. B. Harden in *PCAS* LI (1957), pp. 12–16, pl. iii.

78 FRAGMENT OF BARREL-SHAPED OIL FLASK

Rhenish, late 2nd or early 3rd century AD

Colourless, with opaque yellow trailing; retains 2 of original 4 applied feet supporting horizontal barrel. Preserved L: 7.3 cm. Mus. Arch. Ethn. CAS.1883.798.

From ancient cemetery at Litlington, Cambs. (cf. earlier vessels, **65**). Cambridge Antiquarian Society collection; ex-coll. Webb.

Cf. Fremersdorf, *Denkmäler*, VI, pp. 32–3, pls. 35–9; Harden *et al.*, *Masterpieces*, p. 85 no. 113.

79b, 78, 79a

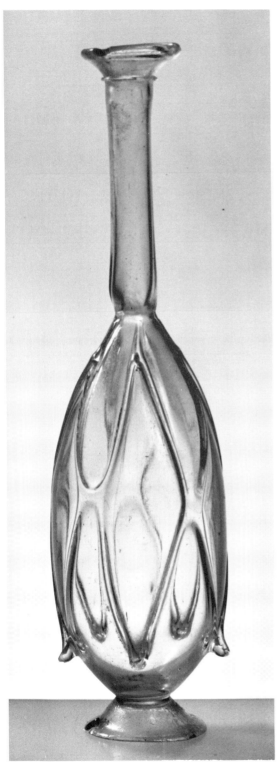

77a

79 LATER VESSELS FROM THE RHINELAND

Rhenish, 3rd and 4th centuries AD

a. Flask, Clear, with greenish tint; flattened underneath; 5 indentations in sides; rim folded in. H: 12.3 cm. Mus. Arch. Ethn. RC.23.739.

From Trier. Ransom collection.

Cf. Hayes, *Toronto*, p. 154 no. 641, pl. xl.

b. Bottle-flask. Clear, with faint greenish tint; pontil mark on base; funnel neck; rim folded down then up again. H: 10.1 cm. Mus. Arch. Ethn. RC. 23. 757.

From Andernach. Ransom collection.

Cf. Isings, *Dated Finds*, p. 120, Form 102*b*; La Baume and Salomonson, *Löffler*, p. 71 no. 256, pl. xxxvii 4.

80 VESSELS FROM GRAVEL HILL FARM, NEAR CAMBRIDGE

Rhenish, 3rd or 4th century AD

Found in 1861 in a stone coffin near Gravel Hill Farm (now the University Farm) between Huntingdon and Madingley Roads (find to be discussed by J. Liversidge in *PCAS* LXVII, 1978). Cambridge Antiquarian Society collection.

a. Bottle-flask. Clear with greenish tint; as **79b**, but with shallower funnel-mouth. H: 13.1 cm. Mus. Arch. Ethn. CAS.1883.766*b*.

As **79b**, q.v. Also 2 other similar vessels from same burial, CAS.1883.766*a, c*.

b. Tall oil-flask. Colourless; flattened base; 3 pairs of thin bands incised on body and 2 broader bands on neck; small 'dolphin' handles; ground rim. H: 10.1 cm. Mus. Arch. Ethn. CAS.1883.767.

Cf. Isings, *Dated Finds*, p. 119, Form 100*a*; Doppelfeld, *Köln*, pl. xliii.

Illustrated overleaf

80b, a   **81**

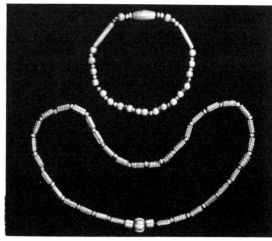

82a, b

81 GOBLET

Northern, *c*. 4th century AD

Clear, with greenish tint; 'cut-out' ring foot with high 'kick'; ground rim. H: 17.3 cm. Mus. Arch. Ethn. Z.21199.

From Amiens. Cambridge Antiquarian Society collection (W. K. Foster bequest, 1891).

Cf. Isings, *Dated Finds*, p. 137, Form 109*b*; Eisen, *Glass*, II, p. 640, pl. clviii, bottom left.

HELLENISTIC AND ROMAN JEWELLERY

Analogous ancient material from different periods and cultures will also be found dealt with separately in this catalogue, viz. Egyptian jewellery and amulets in the Dynastic tradition (**3–5, 17–22**), Phoenician head-amulets (**29**), 'eye', mosaic and *millefiori* beads, etc. (**39, 46**), Phoenician, Greek and Roman seals (**47–50**) and Saxon and Coptic beads and amulets (**112, 114**).

82 TWO NECKLACES

Romano-Egyptian, *c*. 2nd–5th centuries AD (?)

From Egypt. Given by R. G. Gayer-Anderson.

a. Clear metal throughout; gilt spherical, barrel and cylindrical beads and small silvered spherical beads (giving effect of pearls), in most cases with gilding or silvering protected by further layer of colourless metal; restrung. String L: 22.5 cm. EGA.6280.1943.

b. Knobbed cylinder and segmented beads in gilt clear metal (unprotected gold leaf on surface) and silvered 'pearl' beads as on **a**; restrung. String L: 43.0 cm. EGA.6279.1943.

Brunton regarded such gilded and silvered beads as late Ptolemaic or early Roman, but the knobbed beads of **b** seem inspired by late Roman or early Byzantine granulated goldwork; cf. Brunton, *Qau*, III, p. 27, pls xlv 64, xlvi 147–8, 153, 156, 194–200; for knobbed beads, cf. Froehner, *Gréau*, p. 134, no. 962, pl. clxxi 10–11.

83 BRACELETS

Probably all *c*. 4th century AD

a. Coiled from twisted clear rod with thin enclosed 'thread' of green metal. D: 7.3 cm. E.192.1934.

From Egypt (?). Given by Dr G. F. Rogers.

Cf. *QDAP* VIII (1939), pp. 45–50, pl. xxxii 2*d, e*; for early Roman currency of same technique, *cf.* **96**.

b. Deep blue; spun, with tooled serrations on outer edge. D: 5.8 cm. GR.121*b*.1876.

From Cyprus. Cesnola collection.

Cf. *QDAP* I (1939), pp. 3–8, pl. vi 13; *QDAP* III (1934), pp. 81–91, pl. xxiv 2; Harden, *Karanis*, p. 283 nos. 851–4, pl. xxi.

83c, 84c, 83b, 84b, 84a, 83a

c. Iridised deep mauve; 6-ribbed, coiled. D: 6.6 cm. GR.9a.1972.

Given by R. V. Nicholls.

Cf. Platz-Horster, *Berlin*, p. 79 no. 158.

84 FINGER RINGS

From Cyprus (**b** and **c** from Paphos). Cesnola collection and given by Cyprus Exploration Fund.

a. Hellenistic, 4th–2nd centuries BC

Clear, set with convex green-metal 'stone'; moulded. W: 3.3 cm. GR.GL.35.

b. Graeco-Roman, *c.* 1st century BC or 1st century AD

Snake ring in clear metal with faint amber tint; coiled oval rod. H: 1.85 cm. W: 2.2 cm. GR.22. 1888.

c. Roman, *c.* 3rd century AD

Amber, with blue 'stone' on white mount; spun. W: 2.2 cm. GR.43b.1876.

For gold equivalents, cf. F. H. Marshall, *Catalogue of the Finger Rings, Greek, Etruscan and Roman, British Museum* (London, 1907), p. 119 nos. 714-15, pls. xviii–xix, p. 151 no. 936, pl. xxiv, p. 156 nos. 971-2, pl. xxv; for **a** in glass, cf. *ibid.*, p. 230 no. 1568, pl. xxxiv; T. E. Haevernick in *Jahrbuch des römisch-germanischen Zentralmuseums, Mainz* XVI (1969), pp. 175–82, pl. xxi.

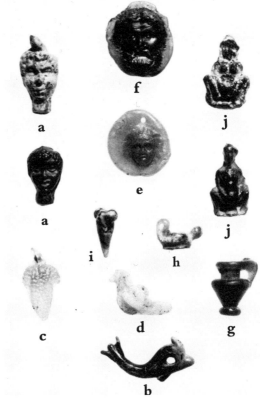

85

85 LATE HELLENISTIC AND ROMAN MOULDED AMULETS

Mainly Egyptian, *c.* 2nd century BC to 4th century AD

From Egypt. Given by Dr M. Bird and R. G. Gayer-Anderson.

a. Negro heads. Black (?). EGA.6219.1943 (H: 2.1 cm), EGA.6236.1943 (H: 1.6 cm).

b. Dolphin. Deep blue. L: 2.65 cm. EGA.6215. 1943.

c. Bunch of grapes. Clear. H: 2.1 cm. EGA. 6225.1943.

d. Dove. White. L: 2.1 cm. EGA.6217b.1943.

e. Disk with Gorgoneion. Bluish green. H: 1.95 cm. EGA.2746.1943.

f. Disk (pin finial?) with bearded head of god on both sides. Blue. H: 2.15 cm. E.307c.1949.

54a, 53, 54b

86

g. Pitcher. Light blue. H: 1.6 cm. EGA.6238. 1943.

h. Lamp. Pale green. L: 1.3 cm. EGA.6239. 1943.

i. Phallus. Checkered mosaic decoration in light blue, red, yellow, deep mauve and white. L: 1.4 cm. EGA.6222.1943.

j. Women in childbirth. Blue. EGA.6235.1943 (H: 2.1 cm), EGA.6234.1943 (H: 1.95 cm).

Cf. Froehner, *Gréau*, pp. 123–4 nos. 850–63, pl. cli.

THE EASTERN PROVINCES OF THE ROMAN EMPIRE

All items are to be understood as free-blown unless otherwise stated.

EGYPT

As the great centre for the production of luxury coloured glass in the old techniques (see above, pp. 24, 26), Egypt seems at first to have played only a very limited part in the development of glass-blowing in the first century AD. But in the later part of that century she seems to have taken the lead in evolving a colourless crystal glass (**33** above may be an early example) and in going on to use this as the medium for splendid facet-cut and engraved decoration, at first on moulded, then on blown vessels. These new techniques were eventually adopted abroad, especially in the Rhineland. The commoner Egyptian blown table glass was, however, usually anything but colourless, but acquired a very distinctive character of its own in late Roman times.

86 BOWL: DUCKLING ON LOTUS BLOSSOM

Egyptian, *c.* early (?) 2nd century AD

Almost colourless; moulded with ring foot and some subsequent tooling; recessed band, 0.8 cm

wide, on top of lip; engraved and facet-cut decoration on exterior: row of oval facets under lip, duckling on lotus flower flanked by lotus buds under foot; on interior, wheel-cut circle around centre medallion. H: 5.9 cm. D: 19.0 cm.

Found in Roman grave II at Girton College, along with **74** and other glass and pottery vessels. Mus. Arch. Ethn., on extended loan from Girton College since 1924.

Pose of duckling still shows influence of Dynastic Egyptian conventions.

Hollingworth and O'Reilly, *Girton*, pp. 32–4 pls. xi–xii; Harden, *Karanis* pp. 66, 119, fig. 1*c*.

Illustrated on p. 45

87 BOWL FRAGMENT: NILOTIC SCENE

Egyptian, 2nd century AD

Colourless; rim ground smooth; engraved and facet-cut decoration on exterior: row of ovals on lip flanked by double line above and single below, frieze with lotus flowers and buds and large fish at shoulder and, beyond this, astragal framed by double lines on both sides. When complete, D: 20.3 cm. Mus. Arch. Ethn. 26.56.

From the Faiyûm. Given by G. D. Hornblower.

Cf. bowl with marine frieze formerly in Zagreb and its counterpart in Cologne: F. Fremersdorf, *Figürlich geschliffene Gläser* (*Römisch-germanische Forschungen*, XIX, Berlin, 1951), pp. 13–15 nos. 21–2, fig. 6, pls. xiii, xiv 1. For fish, cf. *Smith Coll.* p. 181 no. 367; Harden, *Karanis*, p. 87 no. 183, pl. xiii.

87

88 EGYPTIAN TOILET AND TABLE VESSELS

From Egypt. Unknown source and given by J. W. Fell.

a. Toilet bottle, 2nd–3rd centuries AD

Green; pontil mark underneath; lip folded inwards; converted into sprinkler in antiquity by wedging smaller white glass stopper with narrow orifice into neck. H: 19.6 cm. Mus. Arch. Ethn. 66.64.

Cf. Isings, *Dated Finds*, p. 98, Form 82 A(2); Harden, *Karanis*, pp. 265, 267, 272 no. 799, pl. xx.

b. Beaker, 4th–5th centuries AD

Clear bubbly metal with yellowish-green tint; pad base with tooling marks; blue trailed band round body; fire-rounded lip. H: 11.0 cm. Mus. Arch. Ethn. 66.60.

Cf. Brunton, *Qau*, III, p. 28, pls. xlix 12–14, l 6; Harden, *Karanis*, pp. 133–4, 143 nos. 362–4, pl. xv.

c. Jar with open-work zig-zag coil around neck, 4th–5th centuries AD

Clear bubbly metal with pale yellowish-green tint; pad base with tooling traces and pontil mark under; out-turned lip with rim rolled inwards; zig-zag trailing of same metal. H: 8.5 cm. Mus. Arch. Ethn. Z.21156.

Cf. Harden, *Karanis*, pp. 174–5, 180 no. 494, pls. vi, xvii; *Smith Coll.* p. 161 no. 330. Cf. also the Syrian jar, **106**.

d. Fluted jug, *c.* 4th century AD (?)

Metal as **c**, but with deeper green handle; 'kick' under foot; 21 'optic'-moulded 'writhen' ribs on body; rim rolled inwards. H: 10.7 cm. Mus. Arch. Ethn. 66.66.

Form apparently hitherto unrecorded.

88d, c, a, b

89 EGYPTIAN MINIATURE VESSELS

From Egypt. Given by J. W. Fell.

a. Toilet bottle, *c.* 2nd–3rd centuries AD

Blue; lip folded inwards. H: 2.4 cm. Mus. Arch. Ethn. 66.70a.

Cf. Isings, *Dated Finds*, pp. 42–3, Form 28*b*; C. C. Edgar, *Catalogue Général des Antiquités Égyptiennes du Musée de Caire, Graeco-Roman Glass* (Cairo, 1905), pp. 44–5 nos. 32.597, 32.604, pl. vii.

b. Jar, *c.* 2nd–3rd centuries AD

Clear with faint greenish tint; lip folded inwards. H: 2.9 cm. Mus. Arch. Ethn. 66.70*b*.

Cf. Edgar, *Cairo*, p. 29, no. 32.532, pl. iv.

c. Conical lamp, *c.* 4th century AD

Colourless; lip folded inwards. H: 3.3 cm. Mus. Arch. Ethn. 66.70*d*.

Cf. Isings, *Dated Finds*, pp. 130–1, Form 106*d*; Edgar, *Cairo*, p. 67 no. 32.726, pl. ix.

90a, 89a, b, c, 90b

90 SHALLOW BOWLS

Egyptian, 4th–5th centuries AD

From Egypt (?). Given by C. H. Read.

a. Pale amber; pad base showing tooling striations outside and with pontil mark underneath; hollow rim folded out. H: 3.4 cm. D: 15.0 cm. E.13a.1910.

Cf. Edgar, *Cairo*, p. 6 no. 32.432, pl. i; Harden, *Karanis*, pp. 64–5, 72–4 nos. 89–106, pls. ii, xii.

b. Clear, with yellowish-green tint; as **a**, but rather deeper and with more pronounced 'kick' in centre. H: 4.6 cm. D: 14.2 cm. E.13b.1910.

Cf. Edgar, *Cairo*, p. 7 no. 32.426, pl. i; Thomas, *Bomford*, p. 30 no. 128. On dating of such late Egyptian glass, *cf.* also Hayes, *Toronto*, pp. 2–3.

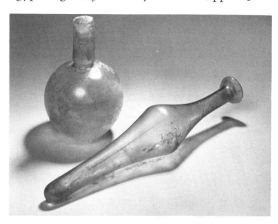

91a, b

THE DANUBE REGION

91 VESSELS FROM ANCIENT MOESIA

Uncertain fabrics, 3rd or 4th century AD

From between Constanţa and Cernavodă in Rumania; acquired with fragmentary toilet bottles of 2nd–3rd century AD (Mus. Arch. Ethn. 1919.11.4, 9). Given by S. Gaselee.

a. Globular flask. Colourless; 'cut-in' constriction at base of neck. H: 17.5 cm. Mus. Arch. Ethn. 1919.11.3.

Cf. Isings, *Dated Finds*, pp. 121–2, Form 103; Spartz, *Kassel*, no. 103, pl. xxv.

b. Spindle-shaped toilet bottle. Clear, with greenish tint; rim rolled inwards, leaving only narrow orifice. H: 35.0 cm. Mus. Arch. Ethn. 1919.11.5.

Cf. Isings, *Dated Finds*, p. 126, Form 105; current earlier in east, cf. C. W. Clairmont, *Excavations at Dura-Europos*, IV, Part v, *The Glass Vessels* (New Haven, 1963), p. 140 no. 736, pl. xxxvi; Froehner, *Gréau*, p. 200 no. 1502, pl. cclxiii 3.

PALESTINE

Palestine clearly had a significant glass industry of its own, but, until recent detailed studies are published, it is not always easy to distinguish confidently its products from those of Syria.

92e, d, a, b, c

92 VESSELS FROM NEAR BETHLEHEM

Palestinian (and Syro-Palestinian?), 3rd–5th centuries AD

A selection from a much larger body of glass of similar date from tombs near Bethlehem. Given by M. Sykes.

a. Funnel-mouthed flask. Clear, with bluish tint, iridised; concave base; lip folded in. H: 18.0 cm. GR.5g.1902.

Cf. Isings, *Dated Finds*, p. 161, Form 133; Hayes, *Toronto*, p. 67 no. 202, pl. xv.

b. Two-handled toilet bottle (amphoriskos). Clear, with amber tint; pale green handles; lip folded in. H: 11.8 cm. GR.5*p*.1902.

Cf. *QDAP* IV (1935), pp. 175–8, pl. lxxxv 1, no. 4.

c. Flask. Clear, with bluish tint; intermittent blue trailing round neck; concave base; fire-rounded rim. H: 13.5 cm. GR.5*c*.1902.

Cf. *QDAP* VI (1937), pp. 153–6, pl. xlii; VIII (1939), pp. 45–50, pls. xxxii 2*f*, *h*, xxxiii 1*a*, *c*.

d. Handled toilet bottle. Clear, with bluish tint; blue handle; 'cut-out' disk base with 'kick' under; rim folded inwards. H: 9.3 cm. GR.5*m*.1902.

Cf. the different, two-handled variety: Hayes, *Toronto*, p. 115 no. 440, pl. xxvii.

e. Dropper or feeder. Clear, with bluish tint; blue trailing on neck; concave base with pontil mark; fire-rounded lip; spout from separate, merged paraison. H: 10.4 cm. GR.5*i*.1902.

Cf. (differently decorated): Thomas, *Bomford*, p. 34 no. 160; Auth, *Newark*, p. 152 no. 199.

SYRIA

The splendid Syrian glass of the first century AD has been dealt with earlier, **51–63**; here the tale is taken up again and continued to late Roman times. Syrian remained one of the richest and most inventive as well as one of the most prolific of glass fabrics. Mould-blown vessels continued, although hardly matching the examples of the first century; and both cut and painted ornament are also attested. Above all, great skill was shown in trailed decoration, which was imitated elsewhere, the 'snake-thread' trailing in particular being copied in the Rhineland.

93 TOILET BOTTLES AND TOILET FLASK

Syrian, second half of 1st and early 2nd centuries AD

From Cyprus. Cesnola collection.

a. From Tremithus. Iridised amber, with paler amber trailing wound 19 times round body and neck; rim folded inwards. H: 6.1 cm. GR.25.1876.

Cf. Hayes, *Toronto*, p. 53 no. 112, pl. ix; Platz-Horster, *Berlin*, p. 55 no. 96.

b. From Amathus. Black with marvered white trailing, giving veined effect; rim folded under, lip flattened. H: 12.3 cm. GR.82.1876.

Cf. Isings, *Dated Finds*, p. 41, Form 28*b*; La Baume and Salomonson, *Löffler*, p. 33 no. 51, pl. v 4.

c. From Golgoi. Blue, with white trailing wound round about 15 times; rounded lip. H: 11.8 cm. GR.65.1876.

93a, b, c

Cf. Hayes, *Toronto*, p. 53 no. 113, pl. ix; A. von Saldern *et al.*, *Oppenländer*, pp. 221–2 nos. 645–6, 648; Thomas, *Bomford*, p. 20 no. 58.

94 WINESKIN-SHAPED TOILET BOTTLE

Syrian, *c.* late 1st century AD (?)
    Heavily iridised clear metal; rim folded inwards; legs pinched out from body. H: 7.6 cm. GR.36. 1876.
    From Cyprus. Cesnola collection.
    Underlying shape of bottle apparently between Isings, *Dated Finds*, p. 24, Form 8, and *ibid.*, p. 42, Form 28*a*.

95 INKWELL

Syrian (?), *c.* 1st–2nd centuries AD
    Clear, with faint greenish-blue tint; 'cut-out' conical foot with 'kick'; 'cut-out' shoulder ridge; rounded edge to central orifice. H: 3.8 cm. D: 4.3 cm. Mus. Arch. Ethn.RC.23.766*b*.
    From Cyprus (?). Ransom collection.
    Dated from close resemblance to pottery ink-wells; cf. F. Oswald and T. D. Pryce, *Introduction to the Study of Terra Sigillata*, pp. 209–10, pl. lxx.
    Cf. von Saldern *et al.*, *Oppenländer*, pp. 242, 248, no. 709. Cf. also cylindrical, hanging and socketed varieties: Auth, *Newark*, p. 119 nos. 145–6; Isings, *Dated Finds*, p. 93, Form 77; Spartz, *Kassel*, no. 35, pl. viii.

96 TOILET STICKS

Syrian, *c.* 1st–2nd centuries AD
    Twisted blue rods with 'thread' of white. L: 19.3, 16.2 cm. GR.58*a*, *c.* 1876.
    From Cyprus. Cesnola collection.
    Function uncertain. Possibly used for mixing and applying cosmetics such as eye-paint.
    Cf. Platz-Horster, *Berlin*, p. 63 nos. 117–18.

95, 96, 94

97 TOILET BOTTLES IN FORM OF DATES

Syrian, late 1st–2nd centuries AD
    From Tremithus in Cyprus. Cesnola collection.
    a. Amber; mould-blown (2-piece mould); rim folded in, lip turned out and flattened. H: 6.2 cm. GR.28.1876.
    b. Iridised amber; as **a**, but with plain, cylindrical mouth with 'knocked-off', fire-rounded rim (resultant heat seems to have caused shoulder to sag after moulding). H: 5.6 cm. GR.22.1876.
    Cf. Isings, *Dated Finds*, p. 94, Form 78*d*; Hayes, *Toronto*, 49 nos. 87–9, pl. vii; Platz-Horster, *Berlin*, pp. 37–8, nos. 50–3.

97a, b

98 PAINTED LIDS

Syrian (or Cypriot?), *c.* 2nd century AD
    Clear metal; blown concave lids with 'knocked-off' edge; painted on interior as follows:

98a

99, 101

a. Head and shoulders of moon-goddess, Selene.
Black outlines; white flesh, drapery, crescent, fillet; red (?) background. D: 6.4 cm. Mus. Arch. Ethn.RC.23.1114.

Probably from Cyprus. Ransom collection.

Cf. O. Vessberg in *Opuscula Archaeologica* VII (1952), pp. 149–50, 180, pl. xxi 2.

b. Standing woman or girl in peplos holding two huge bunches of grapes.

Black outlines; white figure; iridised, with parts of painting lost. D: 7.1 cm. GR.33*b*.1876.

From Tremithus, Cyprus (acquired as lid of earlier jar, **52a**). Cesnola collection.

Cf. *Smith Coll.*, pp. 167–9 no. 344; cf. also examples of Eros with similar grapes, e.g. *JGS* XVI (1974), p. 125 no. 6.

99 DEEP BOWL

Syrian, *c.* 2nd century AD

Colourless body on tall pad foot in green-tinted clear metal with rounded edge and pontil mark under; rounded lip; colourless trailing outside, at angle between body and lip. H: 11.8 cm. D: 20.3 cm. GR.53.1876.

From Neo-Paphos, Cyprus. Cesnola collection.

Cf. Isings, *Dated Finds*, p. 104, Form 87 (which, however, shows 'cut-out' foot); O. Vessberg in *Opuscula Archaeologica* VII (1952), p. 117, pls. ii 15–16, xi 3.

100 FLASK WITH 'SNAKE-THREAD' DECORATION

Syrian, *c.* end of 2nd century AD

Clear, with faint greenish tint; applied coiled base ring; pontil mark under; 4 indents in sides of body; rounded lip; decoration in same metal: trailed bands around neck, convoluted trailed and tooled 'snake-thread' decoration on body. H: 24.2 cm. GR.61.1876.

From Marion in Cyprus. Cesnola collection.

D. B. Harden in *JRS* XXIV (1934), p. 50 no. 3, pl. v; C. Winter, *Treasures of the Fitzwilliam Museum* (London, 1958), pp. 67–9 no. 14, with pl.; *Treasures of Cambridge* (exhibition, Goldsmiths' Hall, London, 1959), no. 437; Brooks, p. 14.

On Syrian 'snake-thread' glass, cf. also C. W. Clairmont, *Excavations at Dura-Europos*, IV, Part V, *The Glass Vessels* (New Haven, 1963), pp. 42–6, pl. xxii.

Illustrated on p. 10

101 TALL BEAKER

Syrian, *c.* 2nd–3rd centuries AD (?)

Pale amber; 'cut-out' foot; 'optic'-formed 'writhen' ribs and 4 indents on body; wheel-cut band below lip. H: 12.6 cm. GR.100.1876.

From Aphrodision in Cyprus. Cesnola collection.

Cf. Isings, *Dated Finds*, pp. 49–50, Form 35; Froehner, *Gréau*, p. 178 no. 1283, pl. ccxlii 3 (no indents); B. Filarska, *Muzeum Narodowe w Warsawie, Szkła Starożytne* (Warsaw, 1952), p. 96 no. 62, pl. xiii (no ribbing).

104

102c, 102a, 103, 102b

102 SMALL JUGS AND FLASK

Syrian, *c.* 2nd–3rd centuries AD

a. Jug. Clear, with faint bluish tint; trailing in same metal; rim folded in; pinched decoration on handle. H: 10.3 cm. GR.119.1876.

From Cyprus. Cesnola collection.

Hayes, *Toronto*, p. 64. Cf. earlier Italian shape: Isings, *Dated Finds*, p. 76, Form 57.

b. Jug. Body colourless, strap handle clear, with bluish tint; 3 wheel-cut bands on body; lip folded in. H: 9.7 cm. GR.25.1955.

From Cyprus. Given by Sir William Elderton.

Cf. (without thumb-rest): Filarska, *Warsaw*, pp. 146–7 no. 140, pl. xxxi 2.

c. Flask. Almost colourless bubbly metal; 8 'optic'-formed (?) ribs; rounded rim. H: 8.5 cm. Mus. Arch. Ethn.RC.23.805*a*.

From Cyprus (?). Ransom collection.

Cf. Froehner, *Gréau*, p. 175 no. 1262, pl. ccxxxviii 3; O. Vessberg in *Opuscula Archaeologica* VII (1952), pl. vii 17.

103 SPOON

Syrian, *c.* 2nd–3rd centuries AD (?)

Clear, with light greenish tint; blown, hollow; pincer mark at pointed tip of bowl. L: 15.5 cm. GR.79.1876.

From Marion in Cyprus. Cesnola collection.

Cf. Harden, *Karanis*, pp. 286–7, fig. 4*m, n, o*; O. Vessberg in *Opuscula Archaeologica* VII, p. 153, pl. x 19; Auth, *Newark*, p. 156 no. 210.

104 CUP WITH FACET-CUT DECORATION

Syrian, under Egyptian influence, *c.* early 3rd century AD

Colourless, with milky iridescence; 2 concentric coils on base, trailed band under lip, all same metal; patterns of narrow oval facets on sides and base and central circular facet under foot; rounded rim. H: 5.8 cm. D: 10.1 cm. Mus. Arch. Ethn. RC.23.788*b*.

From Kourion in Cyprus. Ransom collection.

Harden, *Karanis*, pp. 103, 124, fig. 2*a*. Cf. Isings, *Dated Finds*, pp. 102–3, Form 85*b*.

105a, c, b

107, 106

105 SPRINKLERS AND SMALL FLASK

Syro-Palestinian, *c.* 3rd century AD

Given by Sir William Elderton (except **c**).

a. Sprinkler-flask with honeycomb pattern. Clear, with greenish tint; mould-blown (2-piece mould); deep 'cut-in' sprinkler constriction at base of neck; rim folded in. H: 8.5 cm. GR.29.1955.

On this class of sprinklers, cf. Hayes, *Toronto*, p. 78 nos. 280–1, pl. vii.

b. Sprinkler-flask with net pattern. Translucent pale green metal; technique as **a**. H: 8.5 cm. GR.28.1955

Cf. von Saldern *et al.*, *Oppenländer*, pp. 168, 176 no. 485; Auth, *Newark*, p. 78 no. 80.

c. Funnel-mouthed flask. Colourless, with mauvish iridescence; 'optic'- or mould-formed 'writhen' ribs; lip folded in. H: 8.5 cm. GR.GL.23.

Cf. Spartz, *Kassel*, no. 147, pl. xxxv; Auth, *Newark*, p. 132 no. 152.

106 JAR WITH OPEN-WORK ZIG-ZAG COIL ROUND NECK

Syrian, *c.* late 3rd–4th centuries AD

Clear, with bluish tint; trailed band under lip and zig-zag of same metal; concave base, with pontil mark; rounded lip. H: 7.7 cm. Mus. Arch. Ethn. RC.23.738.

From Cumae in Italy. Ransom collection.

Cf. Hayes, *Toronto*, p. 115 no. 443, pl. xxviii;

Platz-Horster, *Berlin*, pp. 58–9 nos. 106–7. Cf. also the Egyptian footed jar, **88c**.

107 THREE-FOOTED, TWO-HANDLED TOILET BOTTLE

Syro-Palestinian, *c.* 4th century AD

Clear, with bluish-green tint; feet pinched from added wad of metal, reamer and pontil marks under; 'optic'-formed 'writhen' ribbing on body; rounded lip. H: 13.2 cm. GR.GL.20.

Cf. *QDAP* I (1932), pp. 3–9, pl. viii 6.

108 LATE ROMAN JUGS

Syrian and Syro-Palestinian, 4th–5th centuries AD

a. Clear, with greenish tint; mould-blown (2-piece mould): palm branch, large concentric lozenges (twice), lattice, small lozenges (twice); rim folded in. H: 11.6 cm. GR.23.1955.

From near Mount Carmel. Given by Sir William Elderton.

Cf. (from same body moulds?): La Baume and Salomonson, *Löffler*, p. 40, no. 87, pl. x 3; Thomas, *Bomford*, p. 35 no. 168; Auth, *Newark*, p. 81 no. 86.

b. Amber; same-metal strap handle and trailing at neck and under lip; concave base with pontil mark; 'optic'-blown 'writhen' ribbing on body and 10 shallow indents. H: 12.4 cm. GR.24.1955.

108b, c, a   **109**

From Tyre. Given by Sir William Elderton.

Cf. *QDAP* III (1934), pp. 81–91, fig. 24; P. La Baume, *Glas der antiken Welt*, I, *Wissenschaftliche Kataloge des Römisch-Germanischen Museums, Köln*, I (Cologne, 1973), no. D68, pl. xxxii.

c. Clear, with bluish tint; neck trailing and handle in same metal with added 'thread' of deep mauve-blue; pad base with pontil mark under; rim folded inwards. H: 16.4 cm. GR.132.1888.

From Paphos. Given by Cyprus Exploration Fund.

Cf. Isings, *Dated Finds*, p. 155, Form 124*b*; *JGS* XIII (1971), pp. 26–7 no. 48, fig. 47.

109 DOUBLE TOILET BOTTLE

Syro-Palestinian, 4th–5th centuries AD

Clear, with bluish tint; elaborate handles of same metal with added mauve or deep amber 'threads'; green trailed decoration; 2 separately blown bottles, with rims rolled inwards, fused together; pontil wad adhering to bottom. H: 20.6 cm. GR.21.1932.

From Nazareth. Bequeathed by E. Towry-Whyte.

Cf. *QDAP* VI (1937), pp. 54–5, 153–5, pls. vi 6, xlii; *QDAP* VIII (1939), pp. 45–50, pl. xxxii 2*a–c*.

THE DARK AGES

The Romans had not only raised glass to the level of an art form, but had also transformed it from a luxury commodity to a very necessity of life. A measure of their success in the latter respect is the way that its complex technology survived, relatively unimpaired, the destruction of the western Roman Empire and the turmoil of the migration period. In the eastern Mediterranean, the Egyptian and Syrian industries were naturally less directly affected by these catastrophes and maintained considerable continuity for a time, until the Arab conquests of the 7th century brought lasting change. But, in the west, one can but wonder at the way that many of the centres along the Rhine and in northern France continued to produce splendid glass for their new Frankish masters and for a far wider world outside.

THE EAST MEDITERRANEAN

110 SYRO-PALESTINIAN VESSELS

C. 5th–6th centuries AD

a. Hanging lamp. Clear, with bluish tint; pontil mark under; rim folded outwards; 3 suspension loops. H: 5.2 cm. GR.32.1888.

From Paphos, Cyprus. Given by Cyprus Exploration Fund.

Cf. G. M. Crowfoot and D. B. Harden in *JEA* XVII (1931), pp. 196–208, especially p. 199, pl. xxx 40–41; Isings, *Dated Finds*, p. 162, Form 134; Auth, *Newark*, p. 151 no. 197.

110b, a

111a, b

112a, b, c

b. Long-necked flask. Clear, with bluish tint; mould- or 'optic'- blown body with pattern of round projections; concave base; blue trailing wound 19 times round upper neck; broader coiled blue band at rounded lip. H: 19.7 cm. GR.GL.19.

Cf. *QDAP* VIII (1939), pp. 45–50, pl. xxxiii *2a*.

111 EGYPTIAN BOWLS

C. 5th century AD

a. Footed bowl. Clear, with yellowish-green tint; pad foot with tooled surface and pontil mark under; rim bent up and rolled outwards. D: 9.5 cm. E.7.1928.

J. W. L. Glaisher bequest.

Cf. Harden, *Karanis*, pp. 98, 106 no. 228, pls. iii, xiv; Hayes, *Toronto*, p. 142 no. 595, fig. 19, pl. xxxvii.

b. Stemmed bowl. Clear, with amber tint; on stem with flattened tooled disk foot with pontil mark under; rim as **a**. D: 11.8 cm. Mus.Arch. Ethn. 66.58.

From Egypt. J. W. Fell gift.

Cf. Harden, *Karanis*, pp. 127–31, fig. 2*h–k*; Cooney, *British Museum*, p. 106 no. 1091.

112 COPTIC EGYPTIAN BEADS AND AMULETS

C. 5th–6th centuries AD

a. Pendant crosses. Moulded and ground; green metal: E.A.59; clear: E.70.1891, EGA.6230. 1943. H: 1.8–3.1 cm.

From Medînet Habu and elsewhere in Egypt. Given by G. J. Chester and R. G. Gayer-Anderson.

b. Pendant disk: St Menas. Amber; moulded. H: 2.3 cm. GR.106*k*.1876.

From Amathus in Cyprus. Cesnola collection.

c. Necklet. Apart from a few pieces of coral, round beads of opaque green glass and clear drop-shaped pendants with additional sheets of thin colourless metal on back to enclose translucent organic substance (Brunton suggests a resin). As strung, L: 15.8 cm. E.76.1931.

From Tomb 801 at el-Maṭmar (grave of 6-year-old child). Given by British Museum.

G. Brunton, *Matmar* (London, 1948), p. 92, pl. lxvii 9.

113

113 CONICAL BEAKER

Frankish, probably Rhenish, 5th century AD

Bubbly clear metal, with greenish tint; pontil wad under; 'optic'-blown 'writhen' ribbing on body; trailing of same metal some 11 times round under lip; rounded rim. H: 14.8 cm. Mus. Arch. Ethn. 48.1599.

From Anglo-Saxon grave 73, Linton Heath barrow, Cambs. Braybrooke collection.

Hon. R. C. Neville in *Arch J* XI (1854), p. 109, with fig.; Baron J. de Baye, *Industrial Arts of the Anglo-Saxons* (London, 1893), p. 107, pl. xiv 2; Hartshorne, *OEG*, p. 116, fig. 126; D. B. Harden in D. B. Harden, ed., *Dark Age Britain, Studies Presented to E. T. Leeds* (London, 1956), p. 160 no. IIId 2; H. G. Rau in *Festschrift für Waldemar Haberey* (Mainz, 1976), p. 116.

114 NECKLACE OF COLOURED BEADS

Uncertain fabric (eastern and western elements?), early 6th century AD

114

Apart from isolated items of bronze, jet and amber, mainly simple beads of blue glass (including jug amulet of late Roman type), but also several more elaborate types, including cylindrical and rectangular beads in crude mosaic glass in yellow, red and green and 'dumb-bell' beads in clear metal with yellow trailing. As strung, L: 102.0 cm. Mus. Arch. Ethn.Z.7128.

From Anglo-Saxon burial, probably of woman, grave 48 at Holywell Row, Suffolk. Given by Cambridge Antiquarian Society.

T. C. Lethbridge, *Recent Excavations in Anglo-Saxon Cemeteries in Cambridgeshire and Suffolk* (Cambridge, 1931, *CASP* New Series III), pp. 25–8, fig. 12 7–8.

115 DEEP BOWL

Frankish, 6th century AD

Heavily iridised clear metal, now with faint yellowish tint; trailing in same metal; 5 looped trails radiating from slightly concave centre of base and 1 single trail (where space was lacking for 6th loop); thinner trailing coiled some 10 times round neck; rim rolled outwards. H: 8.0 cm. Mus. Arch. Ethn. RC.23.783.

From southern France. Ransom collection.

Cf. F. Rademacher in *Bonner Jahrbücher* CXLVII (1942), pp. 311–14, pls. lxiv 1–2, lxv 2.

116 BELL BEAKER

Frankish, *c.* late 6th or early 7th century AD

Bubbly, clear pale blue metal; pontil mark under; 'optic'-blown ribbing; rounded rim. H: 9.8 cm. Mus. Arch. Ethn.54.370a.

From grave 34 in Anglo-Saxon cemetery at Mitcham, Greater London (formerly Surrey). Given by Col H. F. Bidder.

H. F. Bidder in *Archaeologia* LX (1906), p. 54, fig. 4; D. B. Harden in *Leeds Studies*, p. 161 no. V *b* 4; H. F. Bidder and J. Morris in *Surrey Archaeological Collections* LVI (1959), p. 115, pl. XX 34. Cf. F. Rademacher in *Bonner Jahrbücher* CXLVII (1942), pp. 307–11, pl. lxi 1–4.

117 PALM CUP

Frankish, late 6th or 7th century AD

Translucent pale green metal; mould-blown; on base, cross on sun-disk-like ground from which radiate 12 rays which develop into ribs at sides of vessel; rounded lip. H: 7.2 cm. Mus. Arch. Ethn. RC.23.784.

From Mainz. Ransom collection.

Cf. F. Rademacher in *Bonner Jahrbücher* CXLVII (1942), pp. 301–7, pl. lv 1–3; Doppelfeld, *Köln*, pp. 71–2, pl. clxxiii.

118 BEAKER

Uncertain fabric, late 6th or 7th century AD

Bubbly clear metal with bluish tint; flattened bottom; rounded, slightly inturned rim; decorated with trailing in 4 groups of horizontal bands bounding 2 friezes of overlapping zig-zags (the latter giving the effect of lozenges); trailing in same metal and, on some of zig-zags, in pale amber. H: 18.8 cm. Currently deposited provisionally with Mus. Arch. Ethn.

Found in June 1977 to north-west of Cambridge in roadworks on A604 Cambridge-to-Huntingdon road near Dry Drayton turn-off; presumably from Anglo-Saxon burial, seemingly on site of later gibbet.

Dr D. B. Harden suggests that shape may be transitional to that of bag beaker; on latter, see D. B. Harden in *Leeds Studies*, pp. 143, 163, and in *Arch J* CXXVIII (1971), pp. 87, 91.

Illustrated overleaf

117, 115, 116

118

PART II THE ORIENT

CHINA

From the Chou through the T'ang dynasties glass was used primarily for small objects such as buttons, amulets and plaques, which were moulded and carved (**119–22**). While evidence is scant, there is some indication that larger vessels also were made between the 6th and 10th centuries. Little is known about glass production during the subsequent dynasties until about 1680 when, under the patronage of the Emperor K'ang Hsi, a glass-house directed by Dutch Jesuits was established in Peking. Once the glass-makers overcame the problem of crizzling, or decay due to an excess of alkali in the glass, they concerned themselves primarily with techniques of colouring, achieving glass of brilliantly clear and deep hues (**123, 125–8**) which was then frequently cut and carved in the same manner as the precious stones it often resembled (**124, 125**).

119 PLAQUE FROM A BELT, APRON OR SUIT

Chinese, Han Dynasty (206 BC–AD 220)

Light green glass in imitation of jade; dark green inlay; traces of gold leaf and red lacquer. H: 4 cm. C.133.1946.

Bequeathed by Oscar Raphael.

Cf. BM, OR 1945. 10–17.173, also given by O. Raphael, and purchased by him from Edgar Gutman in 1933; BM, OR 1943.3–13 (1–369), a similar group of objects, see *BMQ*, VIII (1933–4), p. 148.

120 BUTTONS

Chinese, Han dynasty (206 BC–AD 220)

a. Opaque-white glass with moulded decoration. D: 2.6 cm. C.131.1946.

b. Green glass cut as a flower. D: 4.6 cm. C.136. 1946.

Bequeathed by Oscar Raphael.

121 AMULETS

Chinese, Han (206 BC–AD 220) and T'ang (AD 618–906) dynasties

a. Cicada, Han dynasty. Clear, heavily exfoliating. L: 5.9 cm. C.134.1946.

Cf. V & A, C.684.1936; W. B. Honey, 'Early Chinese Glass', *Burlington Magazine* LXXI (Nov. 1937), p. 213 pl. *A*; jade example Fitz. Mus., O.25.1946.

b. Butterfly, T'ang dynasty. Clear, heavily exfoliating. L: 3.8 cm. C.139.1946.

Honey, 'Chinese', pl. *F*.

Bequeathed by Oscar Raphael.

122 ?HAIR ORNAMENT

Chinese, T'ang dynasty (AD 618–906)

Opaque-white glass with two marbled green and white inlays. L: 8.9 cm. C.132.1946.

Bequeathed by Oscar Raphael.

123 CIRCULAR COVERED BOX

Chinese, incised mark of Yung Cheng (1723–35).

Marbled opaque-yellow and -orange glass; moulded and ground. D: 7.5 cm. C.15.1951.

Bequeathed by R. F. Lambe.

124 DISH AND PLATE

Chinese, each with incised mark of Ch'ien Lung (1736–95)

119, 121a, b

59

124b   **125**

a. Amethyst glass; moulded and ground. H: 23.5 cm. C.11.1951.

b. Thick amethyst glass; underside moulded and cut to resemble flower petals. D: 19.5 cm. C.12.1951.

Bequeathed by R. F. Lambe.

125 COVERED JAR

Chinese, probably made in Shantung at Po Shan for the Peking court, period of Ch'ien Lung (1736–95)

Opaque-yellow glass; carved in relief with prunus branches and birds within *ju-i*-shaped panels. H: 12.2 cm. C.51.1936.

Bequeathed by R. Cory.

Cf. Example with incised mark of Ch'ien Lung in R. Soame Jenyns, *Chinese Art* IV (London, 1965), p. 127.

126 HEXAGONAL BOWL

Chinese, 18th or 19th century

Blue glass, moulded and ground; straight-sided with everted lip; prominent pontil mark. H: 7.9 cm. C.14.1951.

Bequeathed by R. F. Lambe.

127 BRUSH POT

Chinese, 19th century

Blue glass; moulded and carved in the shape of a frog with a hollow in its back. H: 7 cm. C.16.1951.

Bequeathed by R. F. Lambe.

128 DISH

Chinese, incised mark of Tao Kuang (1821–50)

Thick, dull-red glass; moulded and ground. D: 16.8 cm. C.13.1951.

Bequeathed by R. F. Lambe.

129 SNUFF BOTTLES

Chinese, 18th–20th centuries

H: 4.6 cm–7.5 cm.

a. Blue cased with white and cut; two *églomisé* panels inset; B.10. **b.** Clear with white flecks, cased with blue, and cut; two *églomisé* panels inset; B.11. **c.** Blue; shallow cutting; B.4. **d.** Blue overlaid with marbled brown; base cut; M.117. **e.** Light blue; R.35. **f.** Brown; M.42. **g.** Clear with transparent-blue casing; cut foot; C.109. **h.** Yellow and red-orange in imitation of realgar; R.28. **i.** As

h but cut in relief with oriental figures in landscape; B.8. **j.** Yellow cased with red; R.50. **k.** Yellow; foot cut; B.29. **l.** Yellow; cutting on shoulders and foot; C.48. **m.** Clear bubbly metal cased with red and cut as a man; C.51. **n.** Blue cased with white; cut with prunus branches; R.33. **o.** White cased with green, pink, amber, red and blue; cut with floral and bird motifs; C.62. **p.** White cased with turquoise; cut, and painted with landscapes and foliage; C.104. **q.** White; cut and enamelled in colours with birds and foliage; C.215. **r.** White; enamelled in colours with foliage and insects; C.97. **s.** White; enamelled in colours with landscapes; C.101. **t.** Green; enamelled in colours with frogs and lilies; C.88. **u.** Clear cased in red and cut with dragons; J.23. **v.** White; cased with brown-green and cut with figures; C.236. **w.** Light green cased with red and cut with dragons; C.76. **x.** Light green in imitation of jade; cut base; M.124.

Given by C. E. Byas, R. Cory, Lady Jenkinson, C. B. Marlay and O. Raphael.

Cf. L. S. Perry, *Chinese Snuff Bottles* (Tokyo, 1960).

ISLAM

The earliest glass produced in the Islamic world followed the traditions established in the ancient world. The founding of the capital of the Abbasid dynasty in Baghdad in the 8th century, however, fostered a more specifically Islamic style. Wheel-cutting and moulding (**130**) of both clear and coloured glass were the first in a series of favoured decorative techniques which culminated in the 13th and 14th centuries with elaborate enamelling and gilding (**132–4**). When Timur captured Damascus in 1400 many craftsmen, including glass-makers, were removed to Samarkand. As a consequence of this loss orders for mosque lamps and perhaps other more common articles were filled by Venetian glass-houses.

The later history of Islamic glass-making begins in the 17th century. Vessels of this period from

130

Shiraz, considered the finest from Persia, were often deep blue in colour (**137**) and were not commonly embellished, although in India gilding and cutting (**140**) were frequently employed. In spite of the continuing existence of glass-houses in both Persia and India during the 18th and 19th centuries there is evidence of Western European production for these markets (**139**).

Weights, stamps and tokens in glass (**136**) were commonly produced from the 8th to the 14th centuries, particularly in Egypt. They were stamped with inscriptions or occasionally with designs and in part continued the tradition of glass coin weights current in Egypt in the Byzantine period.

130 BOTTLE

Syrian, 7th–9th centuries

Blue glass moulded with circular patterns overall; surface heavily eroded; neck damaged. H: 12.8 cm. E.103.1904.

Bequeathed by Frank McClean.

Cf. Klesse, *Glas* no. 34.

131 BOWL

Syrian, 12th century

Pale blue-green glass; rim folded out; high kick in base. D: 12.2 cm. GR.2*a*.1914.

Bequeathed by Sir Henry Bulwer.

Cf. C. J. Lamm, *Das Glas von Samarra* IV (Berlin, 1928), pl. i 18.

132

132 THREE FRAGMENTS FROM BEAKERS

Syrian, 13th–14th centuries

a. Enamelled in blue, white and red, and gilded. Longest dimension: 7 cm. C.1*c*.1940.

Given by Mrs G. Eumorfopoulos; found at Fustat, Cairo.

b. Enamelled in red and white, and gilded. Longest dimension: 6.4 cm. C.1*a*.1940.

Given by Mrs G. Eumorfopoulos.

c. Clear glass with an amber tinge; gilded, and enamelled in red and white with fish. Longest dimension: 5 cm. E.491.1954.

Bequeathed by Sir Robert Greg, no. 547; purchased in Cairo.

Cf. Harden *et al.*, *Masterpieces*, no. 152.

133 MOSQUE LAMP

Syrian, *c.* 1355

Clear bubbly glass with a yellowish tinge; enamelled in blue, red, white and black; six clear lugs for suspension on the body; inscribed around

134

neck with Qur'an, Sura XXIV, 35, and around the body: 'By order of the most noble authority, the Exhalted, the Lordly, the Masterful, holder of the sword, Shaykhu al-Nāsirī'. H: 35.3 cm. C. 4.1949.

Given by the National Art-Collections Fund in commemoration of the centenary of the Museum's opening; ex-coll. Linant Pasha; Rostowitz Bey; John M. Cook.

Probably made for the Emir Saichu, a cup-bearer to the Sultan, for the cloister and mausoleum he built in 1355. *Bulletin de l'Institute Égyptien*, 2 Série, no. 7 (1886), facing p. 144; G. Schmoranz, *Old Oriental Glass Vessels* (London, 1899), p. 73; C. J. Lamm, *Mittelälterliche Gläser aus dem Nahen Osten* (Berlin, 1930), no. 90.

134 SPRINKLER

Syrian, 14th century

Clear glass with greenish tinge; enamelled on the shoulder in blue, red and green with lotus flowers

and the inscription 'Glory to our Lord, the Sultan'; traces of two bands of red enamel around the body. H: 28 cm. L.109.1948.

On loan from Major Raymond Ades.

Cf. Lamm, *Mittelälterliche*, pl. clxii 2.

135   ZOOMORPHIC VESSEL

(?)Syrian, 14th century

Clear, yellowish glass vessel in shape of a camel-like quadruped. H: 10.4 cm. E.10.1942.

Given by the Rev. R. B. Oliver.

136   WEIGHTS, STAMPS AND TOKENS

Egyptian and Syrian (?), 8th–14th centuries

a. Dinar weight of 'Umar b. Ghaylan, governor of Egypt AD 789–90, transparent grass-green; 4.30 g. **b.** Fifty-dirham weight of al-Nu'man b. 'Umar, 8th century, possibly Syria, transparent blue-green; 142.3g. **c.** Disk weight of half a *wuqiyya* or 'ounce', *c.* AD 750, transparent pale bluish-green; 15.71 g. **d.** Vessel stamp from a half *qist* or 'pint' measure of al-Qasim b. 'Ubaydullah, finance director of Egypt AD 734–42, transparent bluish-green. **e.** Vessel stamp from a measure of shelled lentils, 8th century, transparent yellowish-green. **f.** Dirham-weight token or coin weight of the Fatimid Caliph al-Mu'izz, AD 953–73, translucent green; 2.70 g. **g.** Dirham-weight token of al-Hakim, AD 996–1021, translucent green; 2.95g. **h.** Double-dinar-weight token in the name of the Abbasid Caliph al-Nasir, AD 1180–1225, opaque turquoise; 8.56 g. **i.** Token of 'Umar, also inscribed 'at Cairo', 13th or 14th century, translucent purple; 3.00 g.

Given by the Rev. Greville Chester, the Rev. W. G. Searle and Professor W. Robertson Smith.

137

137   SPRINKLER

Persian, Shiraz, 17th–18th century

Blue glass; long neck with spiral ribbing; tubular base ring. H: 41 cm. C.154.1912.

Bequeathed by C. B. Marlay.

Cf. Honey, *Glass*, pl. xxxvii; Harden *et al.*, *Masterpieces*, no. 161.

138   BOTTLES

Persian, Shiraz, 18th–19th centuries

a. Turquoise; flaring lip; sausage-like neck bulging above shoulder; globular body. H: 16.2 cm. C.153.1912.

Bequeathed by C. B. Marlay.

b. Clear; as **a**, and with faint ribbing at shoulder. H: 22.5 cm. C.1.1902.

Given by Captain M. Sykes.

c. Pale green; as **a**, and with pinched decoration at shoulder; high kick. H: 14.3 cm. GR.1.1914.

Bequeathed by Sir Henry Bulwer; found in Cyprus.

138b, c, d, a

Cf. E. Heinemeyer, *Katalogue des Kunstmuseums Düsseldorf, Glas* I (Düsseldorf, 1966), no. 584.
d. Clear; flaring lip; long wrythen neck; pointed kick. H: 23.3 cm. C.155.1912.
Bequeathed by C. B. Marlay.
Cf. *Ibid.*, no. 581.

139 SPRINKLER

Persian, or possibly European for the Persian market, 19th century
Blue glass; twisted ribbed neck; two handles and two spouts; folded lip. H: 16.8 cm. C.178.1975.
Given by Miss E. H. Bolitho; ex-coll. Ivan Napier.

140

139

140 HUQQA BOWL

Indian, *c.* 1700
Clear glass clouded from use; blown, and cut with stylized flowers on the body and foot. H: 18.2 cm. C.128.1975.
Given by Miss E. H. Bolitho; ex-coll. Ivan Napier.
Cf. Gilded green examples, BM, OR 1961.10–16.1, in Harden *et al.*, *Masterpieces* no. 162; *JGS* IV (1962), p. 143 fig. 23.

PART III EUROPE FROM THE RENAIS-SANCE THROUGH THE 17TH CENTURY

VENICE AND NORTHERN EUROPE

In the 15th and 16th centuries Venice achieved ascendency in the glass industry, exporting wares to England, Europe and the Near East. In nearby Murano vessels were blown and moulded in clear soda-lime glass (*cristallo*), opaque-white glass (*lattimo*) and various coloured glass. In the earliest period glass was frequently decorated with enamelling and gilding (**141–43**), techniques borrowed from the Islamic glass-makers. Later, vessels were embellished with diamond-point engraving or with *latticinio* (**148–9**), intricately woven threads of opaque-white glass. By the mid 16th century delicate wines in clear metal, frequently with elaborate winged stems in colours, characterized the Venetian wares.

In Germany and the Netherlands the *façon de Venise* (**159, 161**) was expressed simultaneously with specifically northern styles (**160, 168**). Venetian techniques for decoration were also adopted (**150, 152, 158**) and preference for many persisted after they ceased being fashionable in Venice and after the *façon de Venise* was no longer the popular idiom in the north.

141

141 BOWL

Venetian, *c.* 1500

Pinched ribs; enamelled in red, white, blue and green, and gilded around the lip; trailed and dentilated foot rim. D: 14.5 cm. C.115.1912.

Bequeathed by C. B. Marlay.

Cf. G. Mariacher, *Italian Blown Glass* (London, 1961), pl. xxxiv; R. J. Charleston, 'Types of Glass Imported into the Near East and some Fresh Examples: 15th–16th century', *Festschrift für Peter Wilhelm Meister* (Hamburg, 1975), pp. 245–51 and fig. 1.

142 TAZZA

Venetian, *c.* 1500

Enamelled in the centre with foliate shapes in blue, red and yellow, and gilded; folded foot. D: 22.7 cm. C. 117.1912.

Bequeathed by C. B. Marlay.

Cf. A. Gasparetto, *Il Vetro di Murano* (Venice, 1958), pl. xxxviii, similar enamelling of primarily trefoil forms.

143

143 TAZZA

Venetian, c. 1500

Gilded and enamelled in colours with the winged lion of St Mark; gilded moulded ribs on the underside; folded lip with a gilded band in scale pattern overlaid with enamelled dots below; folded foot with traces of gilding. D: 28.8 cm. C.116.1912.
 Bequeathed by C. B. Marlay.
 Cf. BM, Slade Coll. S.375.

144 EWER

Venetian, 16th century

Brownish glass; trefoil lip; trailed decoration around neck and shoulder; shell handle finial; hollow knop and folded foot. H: 29.9 cm. C.119. 1912.
 Bequeathed by C. B. Marlay.
 Cf. C. Mosel, *Bild-Kataloge des Kestner-Museums Hannover*, II, *Die Glas Sammlung* (Hannover, 1957), pl. iii.

145 SHALLOW WINE GLASS

Venetian or Netherlands, late 16th century

Clear dark metal; moulded lion-mask stem with traces of gilding. H: 15 cm. C.120.1912.
 Bequeathed by C. B. Marlay.
 Cf. the Hague, Gemeentemuseum, OG-9-38, illus. the Hague, Gemeentemuseum, *Glas Door de Eeuwen* (1957), no. 10; V&A, C.215-1936.

146 SHALLOW BOWL

Venetian, 16th century

Decorated with three circuits of blue metal; area below lip possibly originally gilded; high kick; prominent pontil mark. D: 20.4 cm. C.532.1961.
 Bequeathed by D. H. Beves.
 Cf. V&A, C.4394-1859.

145

147 TAZZA

Venetian, late 16th–early 17th century

Moulded bowl with scalloped edge; hollow, wrythen stem. H: 15.7 cm. C.118.1912.
 Bequeathed by C. B. Marlay.
 Cf. V&A, C.2585.1856; Paris, Musée de Cluny, illus. E. Gerspach, *L'Art de la Verrerie* (Paris, 1885), fig. 71.
 Illustrated on p. 70

148 TWO-HANDLED CUP

Venetian, 16th century

Clear, greyish glass; decorated with horizontal *latticinio* bands; *latticinio* foot and scroll handles; opaque-white bands applied in X-shaped configurations at the base of the bowl; folded foot. H: 15.3 cm. C.131.1912.
 Bequeathed by C. B. Marlay.
 Cf. R. Schmidt, *Das Glas* (Berlin, 1912), p. 106, fig. 66.
 Illustrated overleaf

148

150

147

149

149 FLASK

Venetian, 16th century

Decorated overall with *latticinio* bands; four clear lugs for suspension; foot folded up. H. 21 cm. C.134.1912.

Bequeathed by C. B. Marlay.

Cf. A. Nesbitt, *Catalogue of the Collection of Glass formed by Felix Slade, Esq.* (London, 1871), pl. m207.

150 BOBBIN-STEM GOBLET AND COVER

Netherlands, late 16th–17th century

Decorated overall with vertical *latticinio* bands; two clear mereses and clear finial; folded foot. H: 37.1 cm. C.132.1912.

Bequeathed by C. B. Marlay.

Cf. Honey, *Glass*, pl. xxx*b*; Klesse, *Glas* 2nd ed. (Cologne, Kunstgewerbemuseum, 1973), no. 266; R. Chambon, *L'Histoire de la Verrerie en Belgique* (Brussels, 1955), pl. xiv 47.

Illustrated on p. 69

151 GOBLETS

Venetian, late 16th century

a. Weeping glass; lower half of bowl overlaid with amethyst; hollow stem with blue wings. H: 16.4 cm. C.122.1912.

b. Ribbed hollow stem; folded foot. H: 19.8 cm. C.128.1912.

c. As **b.** H: 17.2 cm. C.130.1912.

Bequeathed by C. B. Marlay.

152 COVERED BEAKER

German, second half of 16th century

Clear metal with grey tinge; decorated with marvered bands of opaque-white glass on the foot and cover, vertical opaque-white ribs on lower third of body, and two horizontal bands of *latticinio* each flanked by two opaque-white bands around the middle; clear finial, folded foot. H: 30.4 cm. C.121.1912.

Bequeathed by C. B. Marlay.

153b, a

Cf. R. Schmidt, *Die Gläser der Sammlung Mühsam*, II (Berlin, 1926), no. 16; Harden *et al.*, *Masterpieces* no. 182.

155, 154

153 WINE GLASSES

Venetian or Netherlands, late 16th–17th century
  a. Bowl decorated with white enamel; hollow stem with clear and blue wings; folded foot. H: 18.1 cm. C.123.1912.
  b. Bowl decorated with white enamel; hollow stem with clear and yellow wings; folded foot. H: 15.8 cm. C.125.1912.
  Cf. Cinzano Glass Coll., no. 3.
  Bequeathed by C. B. Marlay.

154 FLUTE

Netherlands, 17th century
  Twisted stem incorporating an opalescent thread; folded foot. H: 29.2 cm. C.151.1912.
  Bequeathed by C. B. Marlay.

155 GOBLET

Netherlands, 17th century
  Hollow knops; folded foot. H: 28.9 cm. C.129.1912.

Bequeathed by C. B. Marlay.
  Cf. B. Klesse, *Glassammlung Helfried Krug* II (Munich, 1965), no. 499.

156 DECANTER

Dutch, or South German, late 17th century
  Bubbly blue-green metal; 16 moulded ribs; pewter neck band and pewter-mounted stopper. H: 27.4 cm. C.11.1911.
  Given by Mrs James Bedford.
  Cf. *Ibid.*, no. 58.

157 TAZZA

Venetian, *c.* 1600
  Clear bubbly glass; centre decorated with two applied and milled cordons of clear glass to either side of an applied turquoise chain; folded foot. D: 27.7 cm. C.1.1925.
  Given by Mrs Leonard Cohen.

71

157

159

A. W. Frothingham in *Spanish Glass* (London, 1963), p. 40 and pl. xi*a*, *b* has assigned this class of object to Barcelona based on numerous diamond-point-engraved examples (cf. G. Boesen, *Venetian Glass at Rosenborg Castle* (Copenhagen, 1960), nos. 11, 97, 98). This attribution remains to be proven conclusively.

158 TWO-HANDLED CUP

Netherlands, 17th century

Amethyst bowl diamond-point engraved with flowers, foliage and a bird; clear foot-rim and handles; opaque-white thread around lip. H: 4.7 cm. C.1.1938.

Bequeathed by Leonard Cunliffe.

Cf. V & A, C.584.1903, pinkish metal; E. Heinemeyer, *Katalogue des Kunstmuseums Düsseldorf, Glas* I (Düsseldorf, 1966), p. 96 no. 299, clear, attrib. to Germany; BM, Slade Coll. S.735, blue.

159 WINE GLASS

Netherlands, 17th century

Crizzled bowl 'nipt-diamond-waies' at base and wheel-engraved with birds and fruiting vines; hollow quatrefoil knop; foot folded and engraved with a band of foliage. H: 14.7 cm. C.458.1961.

Bequeathed by D. H. Beves.

160 BOWL OF A WINE GLASS

Netherlands, 17th century

Diamond-point engraved with cupid and two putti, one carrying wheat sheaves, the other vines and grapes, a garland of foliage below. H: 9.1 cm. C.152a.1912.

Bequeathed by C. B. Marlay.

The iconography probably relates to a theme popular in the Netherlands in the late 16th and 17th centuries, *Sine Cerere et Baccho friget Venus*. Cf. **297**.

161 WINE GLASSES

Netherlands, 17th century

a. Bowl decorated with a single applied thread above spikey gadrooning; flat pincered and twisted stem; folded foot. H: 19.7 cm. C.127.1912.

Bequeathed by C. B. Marlay.

b. Hollow knops; folded foot. H: 18.8 cm. C.148.1975.

Given by Miss E. H. Bolitho; ex-coll. Ivan Napier.

c. Flat, twisted stem with central air column. H: 23.3 cm. C.6.1911.

Given by Mrs James Bedford.

160

164b, a, c

162 TOASTING GLASS

Netherlands, late 17th century

Clear, greyish metal; long solid stem. H: 26.2 cm.
C.7.1911.

Given by Mrs James Bedford.

Cf. R. Chambon, *Belgique*, pl. xxxiii 110;
Cinzano Glass Coll., no. 7.

163 GOBLETS

Netherlands, 17th century

a. Crizzled pinkish glass; blue wings and hollow
stem. H: 16 cm. C.124.1912.

b. Hollow knops; folded foot. H: 20.7 cm.
C.126.1912.

Bequeathed by C. B. Marlay.

163a, b

164 WINGED GOBLETS

Netherlands or Germany, 17th century

a. Cup bowl; stem composed of pincered blue
wings attached to a twisted rod encasing red and
white threads; folded foot. H: 27 cm. C.142.1912.

b. Funnel bowl; stem composed of pincered
clear wings attached to a twisted rod encasing red,
white and blue threads; folded foot. H: 29.3 cm.
C.139.1912.

c. Round-funnel bowl; stem composed of
pincered clear wings attached to a twisted rod
encasing red and white threads; folded foot.
H: 27 cm. C.141.1912.

Bequeathed by C. B. Marlay.

Cf. Klesse, *Glas*, nos. 308–19.

165 WINGED GOBLET AND COVER

Netherlands or Germany, 19th century

Round-funnel bowl; stem composed of pincered
blue wings attached to a twisted rod encasing
yellow, blue, white and red threads; cover finial
composed of similar rods surmounted by a dragon's
head in blue; folded foot. H: 43.8 cm. C.138.1912.

Bequeathed by C. B. Marlay.

To be published in a forthcoming volume of
JGS. For glasses of this type produced in the
1880s–90s by Köln-Ehrenfeld see Klesse, *Glas*,
nos. 520–2 and pls. xxvi, xxvii.

166 TRICK GOBLET

German, late 16th–early 17th century

Clear crizzled and weeping metal; siphon with stag finial; horizontal ridging on bowl; milled cordon around base of bowl; three pincered trails of glass from base of bowl to bottom of pierced, hollow knop; folded foot; left rear leg and right ear of stag broken.

Given by Mrs S. Goetz.

Cf.W. Buckley, *European Glass* (London, 1926), pl. xlib; Klesse, *Glas*, no. 245; Cinzano Glass Coll. no. 55.

167 COVERED GOBLET

Netherlands or Germany, 17th century

Bubbly brownish metal; bowl and cover each decorated with three prunts; hollow knop; folded foot. H: 19.8 cm. C.22.1975.

Given by Miss E. H. Bolitho; ex-coll. Napier.

168 HUMPEN

German, dated 1655

Brownish glass; gilded and enamelled in colours with the arms of Johann Georg II of Saxony, and inscribed 'I.G.H.Z.S.I.C.V.B.C.' and 'Kellerey Lösnitz'; the reverse enamelled with fruiting vines. H: 29.8 cm. C.12.1932.

Given by Mrs W. D. Dickson.

Cf. A. von Saldern, *German Enameled Glass* (Corning, 1965), fig. 355 right, identical arms and inscription, dated 1660.

169 BEAKER

German, 19th century

Brownish glass; enamelled in colours with the arms of Fürstenberg, and the inscription 'COM· DE·FURSTENBERG·1654'; gilded rim. H: 9.3 cm. C.2.1943.

Given by Mrs S. Goetze.

Cf. *ibid.*, pp. 436–8 nos. 159–61.

170 EWER

?Venetian, 19th century

Greyish glass; body decorated overall with vertical *latticinio* bands; clear handle; trefoil lip. H: 29.5 cm. C.133.1912.

Bequeathed by C. B. Marlay.

166

168

74

ENGLAND

In 1574 Jacopo Verzelini, a Venetian glass-maker, received a patent to produce *cristallo* in London. Nine examples of his glass, dated between 1577 and 1590, have thus far been identified. The Fitzwilliam's goblet (**171**) is therefore of particular importance as one of this small group which represents the earliest English glass that is dated and that can be attributed securely.

171

Glass in the Venetian manner continued to be produced in England after Verzelini and through to the beginning of the 18th century. By the 1670s, however, the preference for a new, more reserved style became apparent. Between 1667 and 1673 John Greene, London glass seller and importer, ordered from Murano glasses which, it is known from Greene's extant drawings, were to be uncomplicated, sturdy and stable, yet elegant in form (**187**), precursors of the baluster-stem goblet of the 18th century.

With George Ravenscroft's development of lead-glass around 1675–6, the English fabric achieved international importance. The clear, heavy and light-refractive metal, while not easily adapted to the delicate Venetian shapes, was particularly well suited to cutting and to the new heavier styles (**174**). In the process of refining his formula for 'christalline' glass, Ravenscroft inadvertently produced a material which crizzled. To mark his presumed triumph over this problem he began stamping his vessels with a raven's-head seal. This act was premature as crizzled sealed pieces exist (**173**).

171 GOBLET

English, London, glass-house of Jacopo Verzelini, dated 1578

Dark soda-glass; diamond-point engraved, probably by Anthony de Lysle, with a frieze of hounds, a stag and a unicorn, and with the initials AT and RT and the date in three panels within a frieze of foliage; foliate design engraved on the foot. H: 21.6 cm. C.4.1967.

171

174

175

Given by the Friends of the Fitzwilliam; ex-coll. Commander Sir Hugh Dawson.

The Fitzwilliam goblet is the earliest attributed to Verzelini but for the goblet in the Corning (NY) Mus. of Glass dated 1577. V &A, *International Art Treasures Exhibition, Catalogue*, no. 501, pl. cclxxv; R. J. Charleston, 'Twenty-five Years of Glass Collecting', *Conn.* CL (June 1962), p. 121 fig. 1; V &A, *Circle of Glass Collectors Commemorative Exhibition 1937–1962, Catalogue* (1962), no. 102 and pl. i; *English Glass, Catalogue*, no. 1; R. J. Charleston, *English Glass* (London, V &A Museum, 1968), no. 1 and figs. 1–2; *JGS* x (1968), p. 168 fig. 45; cf. W. A. Thorpe, 'The Lisley Group of Elizabethan Glasses', *Conn.* CXXII no. 510 (Dec. 1948), pp. 110–17, figs. 5–7, and subsequent correspondence between W. A. Thorpe and B. Perret, *Conn.* CXXIII no. 511 (March 1949), p. 56; E. S. Godfrey, *The Development of English Glassmaking 1560–1640* (Oxford, 1975).

Illustrated also on frontispiece

172

172 STANDING DISH

English, *c.* 1670

Bubbly soda-glass; 'wrythen' mould-blown ribbing; folded foot and rim. D: 32.9 cm. C.623. 1961.

Bequeathed by D. H. Beves.

E. B. Haynes, 'Some Pre-Ravenscroft Glasses', *Conn.* CXXV (May 1950), p. 89 fig. 6; RA, *The Age of Charles II* (1960–61), no. 318; *Glass Circle Cat.*, no. 110.

177

173 BOWL AND STAND

English, Savoy glass-house of George Ravenscroft, *c.* 1676–7

Crizzled lead-glass; bowl and stand with 'wrythen' rib-moulding; raven's-head seal on milled cordon around base of bowl; rim of bowl and of stand folded. D: (of bowl) 17.8 cm; (of stand) 24.1 cm. C.612a–b.1961).

Bequeathed by D. H. Beves.

Charleston, 'Cambridge', p. 33 fig. 3; Charleston, 'Twenty-five Years', fig. 122; RA, *Charles II*, no. 317; *Glass Circle Cat.*, no. 112 and pl. ivb; R. J. Charleston, 'Some Important Early English Glasses, Part I', *Antiques* LXXXVIII (Jan. 1963), p. 93 fig. 4; D. C. Davis, *English and Irish Antique Glasses* (London, 1964), fig. 1 bowl only; J. P. Hudson, 'George Ravenscroft and his Contribution to English Glassmaking', *Antiques* XCII (Dec. 1967), p. 826 no. 14; R. J. Charleston, 'George Ravenscroft, New Light on the Development of his "Christalline Glasses"', *JGS* x (1968), p. 163 fig. 2; *English Glass Cat.*, no. 21; Charleston, *English Glass*, no. 11, fig. 11. Cf. Sydney, Australia, Coll. G. Gordon Russell, bowl only, D: 17.5 cm, faintly crizzled, see *JGS* VI (1964), p. 166 fig. 45.

174 POSSET POT

English, Savoy glass-house of George Ravenscroft *c.* 1677–8

Faintly crizzled lead-glass; raven's-head seal at base of the spout; gadrooned base. H: 7 cm. C.564.1961.

Bequeathed by D. H. Beves.

Charleston, 'Cambridge', p. 33 fig. 2; RA, *Charles II*, no. 319; *Glass Circle Cat.*, no. 111, pl. iv*a*; Charleston, 'Early Glasses', p. 93 fig. 2; Hudson, 'Ravenscroft', p. 825 no. 7; Charleston, 'Ravenscroft', p. 167 fig. 18; *English Glass Cat.*, no. 25; Charleston, *English Glass*, no. 10 fig. 10.

Illustrated on p. 76

175 POSSET POT

English, probably from the Stony Street, South-wark Glass-house, *c.* 1680

Heavily crizzled lead-glass; sealed at the base of the spout with an S. H: 8.5 cm. C.650.1961.

Bequeathed by D. H. Beves; ex-coll. Sir Hugh Dawson; originally from Ham House.

Glass Circle Cat., no. 116; Charleston, 'Early Glasses', p. 93; *English Glass Cat.*, no. 27; Charleston, *English Glass*, no. 18 fig. 18. For the only other known examples marked with the S seal see V &A, C.589.1925, stem of a wine glass with S seal, and London, Coll. Barry Richards Esq., crizzled goblet similarly sealed; see Buckley, *OEG*, pp. 24 and 30, and Thorpe, *A History*, pp. 138–9, for discussion of this class of object.

Illustrated on p. 77

176

176 WATER GLASS

English, *c.* 1690

Heavy clear lead-glass; gadrooning around base. H: 8.7 cm. C.662.1961.

Bequeathed by C. B. Marlay.

Shape and gadrooning relate this glass to Ravenscroft's sealed posset pots.

173

178

179

177 PLATTER

English, possibly from the Henley-on-Thames or Savoy glass-house of George Ravenscroft, *c.* 1674–6

Crizzled lead-glass; moulded ribs; folded rim. D: 28.8 cm. C.294.1961.

Bequeathed by D. H. Beeves.

Hudson, 'Ravenscroft', p.831 fig. 34.

Illustrated on p. 78

178 DOUBLE CUP OR SWEETMEAT

English, possibly from the Savoy glass-house of George Ravenscroft, or his successor Hawley Bishopp, *c.* 1680

Clear lead-glass; heavily gadrooned above and below hollow quatrefoil knop; folded foot and rim. H: 11.4 cm. C.596.1961.

Bequeathed by D. H. Beves; ex-coll. C. Kirby Mason.

Buckley, *OEG*, pl. xi left. Cf. Museum of London, single cup said to have been found with two sealed Ravenscroft pieces, Charleston, *English Glass*, no. 17, fig. 17.

179 ROEMER

English, possibly from a glass-house of George Ravenscroft or his successor Hawley Bishopp, *c.* 1680

Clear lead-glass; chain trailing on bowl above heavy gadrooning; trailed collar between bowl and stem; hollow stem with 'raspberry' prunts; folded foot. H: 24.7 cm. C.295.1961.

Bequeathed by D. H. Beves.

Cf. Warsaw Roemer of George Ravenscroft, Warsaw, Muzeum Narodowe, thought to have been made for the visit of King John III Sobieski to Danzig in 1677–8, H: 27.3 cm, Charleston, 'Ravenscroft', p. 164 figs. 5–8; Toledo, Mus.Art. no. 54.15, illus. *Art in Glass* (Toledo, 1969), p. 62.

180 EWER

English or possibly French, *c.* 1680

Crizzled glass; helmet-shaped body; foot folded up. H: 21.4 cm. C.472.1961.

Bequeathed by D. H. Beves.

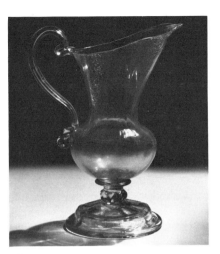

180

181 DECANTER JUG AND STOPPER

English, *c.* 1680

Clear lead-glass; hollow stopper with ball finial above moulded gadrooning; trailing at neck and shoulder; chain trailing around belly; moulded vertical ribs over lower half of body; thick plain foot; handle with thumb-piece. H: 29.9 cm. C. 293.1961.

Bequeathed by D. H. Beves.

Cf. J. Hayes, *The Garton Collection of English Table Glass* (London, 1965), p. 16 fig. 5.

181

182 DECANTER JUG

English, *c.* 1680

Yellowish glass; 'nipt-diamond-waies' over body; six columns of applied, pincered decoration; vertical mould-blown ribbing from lip to shoulder; vermicular collar; tooled foot. H: 19.4 cm. C.496.1961.

Bequeathed by D. H. Beves.

Hudson, 'Ravenscroft', p. 829 fig. 26; cf. Corning (NY) Mus. of Glass, *ibid.*, p. 828 fig. 23.

183 CRUET

English, *c.* 1680

Slightly yellowish glass; 'nipt-diamond-waies' and five columns of pincered decoration on body; beak-like finial on spout; hollow handle with trailed pincered decoration; tooled foot. H: 10.2 cm. C.652.1961.

Bequeathed by D. H. Beves.

Cf. **182**.

182

184 DECANTER AND STOPPER

English, *c.* 1685

Heavily crizzled lead-glass; moulded prunts and applied arcading around body; gadrooning at base;

184

186

long neck with string rim and loop handle; solid tapering stopper with milled top. H: 30.7 cm. C.604.1961.

Bequeathed by D. H. Beves.

Charleston, 'Cambridge', p. 37 fig. 24; RA, *Charles II*, no. 309; *Glass Circle Cat.*, no. 127.

185   WINE GLASS

English, 17th century

Bubbly, greyish soda-glass; moulded gadrooning at base of bowl; ribbed hollow knop; folded foot. H: 16.3 cm. C.305.1961.

Bequeathed by D. H. Beves; ex-coll. C. Kirby Mason.

Thorpe, *A History*, pl. viii 1.

186   WINE GLASS

English or Netherlands, *c.* 1670

Yellowish soda-glass; horizontal 'Lynn' rings and spikey gadrooning on bowl; ribbed hollow stem. H: 14.1 cm. C.21.1975.

Given by Miss E. H. Bolitho; ex-coll. Ivan Napier.

Glass Circle Cat., no. 103; Charleston, 'Early Glasses', p. 92; *English Glass Cat.*, no. 10; Charleston, *English Glass*, no. 8, fig. 8; R. J. Charleston, 'A Panoply of English Glass', *Country Life*, CLXVIII (4 July 1968), p. 38 fig. 3.

187   WINE OR ALE GLASS

English, or Venetian for the English market, *c.* 1670

Yellowish soda-glass; hollow knop; folded foot. H: 20.2 cm. C.474.1961.

Bequeathed by D. H. Beves; ex-colls. C. Kirby Mason, Henry Brown.

The shape of this glass relates closely to drawings in the letters dating 1667–73 from the London glass seller and importer John Greene to his Venetian supplier Allesio Morelli (BM, Sloane Ms. 857). Thorpe, *A History*, pl. viii 3; RA, *Charles II*, no. 332; *Glass Circle Cat.*, no. 109; *English Glass Cat.*, no. 12.

188   WINE GLASS

English, or possibly Netherlands, *c.* 1680

Soda-glass; hollow quatrefoil knop; folded foot. H: 13.8 cm. C.407.1961.

187

Bequeathed by D. H. Beves.
Cf. Dutch-engraved example, V &A 5237-1901; lead-glass example, Haynes, *Glass*, pl. lvie.

189, 188

189 WINE GLASS

English, *c.* 1680
    Yellowish soda-glass; 'nipt-diamond-waies' on bowl; hollow quatrefoil knop; ribbed and folded foot. H: 13.8 cm. C.595.1961.
    Bequeathed by D. H. Beves.
    A similar example in crizzled lead-glass has been attributed to the Savoy glass-house of George

Ravenscroft, see *Glass Circle Cat.*, no. 124; Charleston, 'Early Glasses', p. 94 fig. 9.

190 GOBLET

English, *c.* 1690
    Yellowish soda-glass; diamond-point engraved with foliage, a peacock and a peahen; hollow knop contains a William III sixpence dated 1690; folded foot. H: 18 cm. C.520.1961.
    Bequeathed by D. H. Beves; ex-colls. C. Kirby Mason, Henry Brown.
    Thorpe, *English and Irish*, fig. 50 left; *Glass Circle Cat.*, no. 131.

191 GOBLET

English, or possibly Netherlands, *c.* 1690
    Soda-glass; diamond-point engraved with birds and foliage; hollow dumb-bell stem; folded foot. H. 14.2 cm. C.475.1961.
    Bequeathed by D. H. Beves; ex-coll. Col R. F. Ratcliffe.
    Thorpe, *A History*, pl. v; *Glass Circle Cat.*, no. 108; cf. R. J. Charleston, 'Dutch Decoration of English Glass', *TSGT* xli (1957), p. 232 fig. 2.

190

197

193a, b

192 GOBLET

English, late 17th century
 Yellowish-brown soda-glass; hollow dumb-bell stem; folded foot. H: 12.9 cm. C.615.1961.
 Bequeathed by D. H. Beves.

193 WINES

a. Netherlands or possibly English, *c.* 1680
 Soda-glass; 'nipt-diamond-waies' at base of bowl; two hollow quatrefoil knops; folded foot. H: 18.1 cm. C.551.1961.
  b. English, *c.* 1680
 Lead-glass; 'nipt-diamond-waies' at base of bowl; single hollow quatrefoil knop. H: 15.3 cm. C.307.1961.
 Bequeathed by D. H. Beves.

194 WINE GLASS

English, late 17th century
 Lead-glass; spikey gadrooning around bowl; four pincered vestigial wings at top of stem; folded foot. H: 13.4 cm. C.398.1961.
 Bequeathed by D. H. Beves.

195 WINE GLASS

English, late 17th century
 Lead-glass; dimpled and rib-moulded bowl; six pincered wings at top of stem; folded foot. H: 14.2 cm. C.490.1961.
 Bequeathed by D. H. Beves.
 Cf. Buckley, *OEG*, pl. x right.

196 WINE GLASS

English, late 17th century
 Lead-glass; waisted bowl with six pincered wings at base; five pincered wings at top of stem; deeply folded foot. H: 13.2 cm. C.481.1961.
 Bequeathed by D. H. Beves; ex-coll. C. Kirby Mason.
 Ibid., pl. xi centre.

197 POSSET POT AND COVER

English, late 17th century
 Gadrooned base; a circuit of 'raspberry' prunts between applied threads around the body; winged handles; cover with 'raspberry' prunts, gadrooning and an elaborate crown finial; damaged and repaired. H: 27.5 cm. C.211.1961.
 Bequeathed by D. H. Beves.
 W. A. Thorpe, *English Glass* (London, 1935), p. 181 and pl. xviia; Charleston, 'Cambridge', p. 37 no. 23; RA, *Charles II*, no. 316; *Glass Circle Cat.*, no. 150; Charleston, 'Early Glasses', p. 94 fig. 10; *English Glass Cat.*, no. 66; Charleston, *English Glass*, no. 28, fig. 28.

198 POSSET POT AND COVER

English, late 17th century
 Heavy gadrooning around base of bowl and around cover; two circuits of moulded face masks and roses, one around the body and one on the cover; trailed decoration on handles; four short

199

damaged spires at finial; body of vessel broken and repaired. H: 28.5 cm. C.606.1961.

Bequeathed by D. H. Beves.

Hartshorne, *OEG*, pl. xxxiii; Brooks, p. 38.

199 CEREMONIAL GOBLET AND COVER

English, late 17th century

Clear lead-glass; heavy, moulded gadrooning on base of bowl and on cover; figure-of-eight stem; folded foot; cover finial composed of trailed and dentilated scrolls to either side of a tall spire constructed of a series of knops. H: 53.8 cm. C.608.1961.

Bequeathed by D. H. Beves.

Charleston, 'Cambridge', p. 34 fig. 9; RA, *Charles II*, no. 313; *Glass Circle Cat.*, no. 130; *English Glass Cat.*, no. 55; Charleston, *English Glass*, no. 30, fig. 30; G. Mills, *English and Irish Glass, Commemorative Goblets* (Guildford, 1965), p. 9 fig. 8; Brooks, p. 36.

200 CEREMONIAL GOBLET AND COVER

English, late 17th century

Bowl restored; original 'raspberry' and rose prunts between filets around bowl and cover; original heavy moulded gadrooning at base of bowl and on cover; three-sectioned hollow stem; folded foot; crown finial with twisted spire at the top. H. 56.5 cm. C.377.1961.

Bequeathed by D. H. Beves.

Glass Circle Cat., no. 129.

201 CEREMONIAL GOBLET AND COVER

English, late 17th century

Heavy gadrooning at base of bowl and on cover; three hollow knops separated by clear mereses, central knop with spiral fluting; folded foot; cover

200

210 bis COMPOSITE STEMS

English, mid 18th century

a. Wine glass. Trumpet bowl and foot engraved with fruiting vines. Air-twist over plain stem section, beaded knop between. H: 17.5 cm. C.628.1961.

b. Champagne glass. Double-ogee bowl; air-twist over plain stem section, beaded knop between. H: 14.2 cm. C.438.1961.

Bequeathed by D. H. Beves.

295

296

297

THE CONTINENT

ENGRAVED GLASS

The development of potash-lime-glass in Germany and Bohemia occurred nearly simultaneously with the development of lead-glass in England. Like its English counterpart, the new continental glass was clearer and heavier than the Venetian *cristallo* and gave rise to more substantial baroque forms. It was particularly well suited to wheel-engraving, a technique previously used with great distinction in Bohemia for cutting and decorating hard stones. By the end of the 17th century glass engraving, which had flourished in Prague, was thriving in Germany where, in the 18th century, it continued to be the principal means of glass decoration (**300**).

295 GOBLET

Probably English, engraved by Frans Greenwood, Dordrecht, Holland, *c.* 1730–40

Bowl stipple-engraved after Antonio Tempesta (1555–1630) with a rearing horse in a landscape;

light baluster stem; foot a replacement. H: 24.9 cm. C.8.1963.

Bequeathed by W. A. Evill.

V & A, *Circle of Glass Collectors Commemorative Exhibition 1937–1962, Catalogue* (1962), no. 304; cf. Amsterdam, Rijksmuseum, no. 16529, dated 1722, and signed, illus. E. Schrijver, *Glas en Kristal* (Bussum, 1961), pl. xiv*b*; Amsterdam, Coll. A. Vecht, dated 1741, inscribed 'Vrijheid' (freedom); F. Hudig, 'Diamond Engraving', in W. Buckley, *European Glass* (London, 1926), pp. xiv–xxxiv.

Illustrated on p. 113

296 GOBLET

English, Dutch engraving, *c.* 1740

Bowl wheel-engraved with an allegory of peace, and on the reverse with the arms of Orange-Nassau and the inscription 'PAX UNA TRIUMPHIS INNUMERIS POTIOR · 11 · APRIL · 1713'; plain stem with tear; foot folded. H: 20.8 cm. C.138. 1975.

Given by Miss E. H. Bolitho; ex-coll. Ivan Napier.

298

300

Engraved to commemorate the Treaty of Pragmatic Sanction. See R. J. Charleston, 'Dutch Decoration of English Glass', *TSGT*, XLI (1957), pp. 229–43.

297 WINE GLASS

English, Dutch engraving, *c.* 1740
Bowl wheel-engraved with a fruiting vine flanked by Bacchus on the left and Venus and Cupid on the right; inscribed above: 'QUI · CAPIT · ILLE · FACIT', and below 'SINE CERERE ET BACCHO FRIGET VENUS'. H: 15.1 cm. C.46.1933.
Bequeathed by the Rev. A. V. Valentine Richards.

298 FRIENDSHIP WINE GLASS

English, Dutch engraving, mid 18th century
Bowl wheel-engraved with clasped hands sur-

rounded by rococo arabesque motifs; light baluster stem. H: 18.2 cm. C.70.1975.
Given by Miss E. H. Bolitho; ex-coll. Ivan Napier.

299 WINE GLASS

English, engraving possibly continental, *c.* 1750
Bowl wheel-engraved with arabesques; air-twist stem. H: 17.5 cm. C.463.1961.
Bequeathed by D. H. Beves.

300 GOBLET

Bohemian, *c.* 1700
Faceted bowl wheel-engraved with floral motifs, birds and putti; base of bowl and one knop cut; upper side of foot wheel-engraved with a band of foliage. H: 19.2 cm. C.149.1912.
Bequeathed by C. B. Marlay.
A glass engraved by the same hand has been

301

116

302

304, 306

attrib. to Georg Schwanhardt the Elder. However, this attribution remains problematical. See E. Meyer-Heisig, *Der Nürnberger Glasschnitt des 17. Jahrhunderts* (Nuremberg, 1963), p. 76 no. 14, pl. WT xiv. For a glass of similar shape and proportion, see E. Heinemeyer, *Katalogue des Kunstmuseums Düsseldorf, Glas I* (Düsseldorf, 1966), no. 331.

301 WINE GLASS

German, Nuremberg, *c.* 1700

Bowl wheel-engraved in three panels with martial subjects: a cavalry man and canon; bugles and drums; and a charging mounted gunman. Inscribed '1 STVCK V CARTAVNEN KNALL/ 2PAVCKEN V TROMPETEN SCHALL/ 3EDLE RITTER LIEBEN ALL'.
Folded foot. H: 14.3 cm. C.144.1912.
Bequeathed by C. B. Marlay.

302 WINE GLASS

Saxony, second quarter of 18th century, Dutch engraving

Bowl wheel-engraved with a domestic scene, and inscribed 'DAT ONS WEL MAG GAAN IN ONSE DAGEN'; lower quarter of bowl, and hollow knop cut. H: 19.9 cm. C.145.1912.
Bequeathed by C. B. Marlay.

303 WINE GLASSES

a. German, first half of 18th century
Bowl wheel-engraved with floral motifs; eight-sided pedestal stem; folded foot. H: 15.8 cm. C.147.1912.
b. Bohemian, first half of 18th century
Bowl wheel-engraved; stem and lower quarter of bowl cut, stem possibly re-cut. H: 16.9 cm. C.150.1912.
c. German, first half of 18th century
Bowl wheel-engraved with floral motifs; eight-sided pedestal stem; folded foot. H: 15.7 cm. C.146.1912.
Bequeathed by C. B. Marlay.

305

307

Cf. Pelham Manor, NY, Coll. R. von Strasser, no. 252 and A. von Saldern, 'Zwischengoldgläser mit Marmorierter Lackbemalung', *Anzeigen des Germanischen Nationalmuseums*, 1976, pp. 133–42.
Illustrated on p. 117

OTHER GLASS

Enamelling in black as well as in colours continued in popularity on the continent and by the end of the first quarter of the 18th century subjects painted in the delicate rococo style as well as in freer and more naive styles appeared on clear and opaque-white glass (**308**, **313**). In Central Europe the ancient technique of sandwiching a layer of gold leaf engraved with a scene between two layers of glass, *Zwischengoldglas*, was revived (**305**, **306**), while in Spain, Bohemia, the Netherlands, France and England lampwork, in which rods of glass were heated over a lamp and twisted into filigree baskets, was also in use (**312**).

304 PLATE

Silesian, early 18th century
    Reverse gilded and painted in colours in a marbled pattern. D: 24.2 cm. C.1.1942.
    Given by Louis C. G. Clarke.

305 *ZWISCHENGOLD* GOBLET

Bohemian, mid 18th century
    Bowl decorated with a battle scene in gold leaf between two sections of clear glass, the outer section faceted; cut stem and foot. H: 20.4 cm. C.1.1934.
    Given by Lady Cohen.
    Cf. Klesse, *Glas*, nos. 384–5.

306 *ZWISCHENGOLD* TUMBLER

Bohemian, mid 18th century
    Gold and silver leaf, and red and green lacquer foliate design between two sections of clear glass; outer section faceted. H: 8.7 cm. C.3.1943.
    Given by Mrs S. Goetz.
    Cf. *Ibid.*, no. 450.
    Illustrated on p. 117

308

307 SHELL SWEETMEAT

Bohemian, c. 1720

Moulded and cut bowl; stem and underside of foot cut. H: 10.5 cm. C.7.1977.

Napier Duplicates Fund.

Cf. Prague, Umĕlecko Průmyslové Muzeum, Česko SKLO (1970), no. 456; Klesse, *Glas*, no. 380.

308 TUMBLER

Silesian, second half of 18th century

Faceted; enamelled in purple and white with a battle scene, the reverse with a single sprig of flowers; underside of foot decorated with six oval cuts in a floral pattern. H: 9.4 cm. C.12.1977.

Napier Duplicates Fund.

Cf. E. Heinemeyer, *Katalogue des Kunstmuseums Düsseldorf, Glas I* (Düsseldorf, 1966), no. 199.

309 DECORATIVE SPOON

French, 19th century

Cut bowl; stem composed of sections of coloured canes; human-head finial in white, black and red. L: 29 cm. C.13.1928.

Bequeathed by Dr J. W. L. Glaisher.

310 FIGURES

French, probably Nevers, 18th–19th centuries

a. Shepherdess: white, brown, yellow, rose and green. H: 12.3 cm. C.1d.1928; **b.** Gentleman: yellow, white, dark blue, turquoise, black, brown and rose. H: 12.7 cm. C.1e.1928; **c.** Ceres or Summer: white, blue, yellow, rose and clear. H: 10.9 cm. C.1p.1928.

Bequeathed by Dr J. W. L. Glaisher.

311 BRANDY BOTTLE

Central European, 18th century

Mould-blown; enamelled with foliage and birds in red, blue, yellow and white; pewter cap. H: 16.6 cm. C.148.1912.

Bequeathed by C. B. Marlay.

Cf. A. von Saldern, *German Enameled Glass* (Corning, 1965), pp. 416–17.

Illustrated overleaf

312 LAMPWORK FRUIT BASKET

Probably Liège, 18th century

Honeycomb-moulded base with high kick; pincered detail. H: 8 cm. C.300.1961.

Bequeathed by D. H. Beves.

Baskets of this type are thought also to have been made in Spain, Bohemia and England. Cf. R. Chambon, *L'Histoire de la Verrerie en Belgique* (Brussels, 1955), pl. xxxvi, no. 128; A. W. Frothingham, *Spanish Glass* (London, 1963), fig. 43; Prague, *Česko SKLO*, no. 51; V&A C.4424-1901.

Illustrated overleaf

311

312

313 OPAQUE-WHITE TUMBLER

Spanish, or possibly Bohemian, *c.* 1788

    Enamelled in blue, yellow, red, green and black with the arms of Castille-León, and inscribed on the reverse 'VIVA CARLOS IV/ Rey de Espana'. H: 14.9 cm. C.13.1977.

    Applied Arts Fund.

    Cf. BM, 73, 5-2, 98.

PART V   THE 19TH AND 20TH CENTURIES

At the beginning of the 19th century Britain continued to set the tone of the European glass industry. The deeply cut glass associated with Ireland was imitated in Europe and perhaps in part provided the impetus for American glass-makers to invent an inexpensive method for moulding glass after this style.

    By the middle of the century continental styles became popular in England. Casing, or layering of different colours of glass, combined with cutting and engraving, techniques in which the Germans and Bohemians excelled, was soon adopted (**317, 318**). Rock crystal carving (**315**) and the *façon de Venise* (**325**) were revived while decoration loosely based on ancient sources (**316**) came into frequent use. Concurrently, the Arts and Crafts Movement reacted strongly against the deep cutting of the late 18th and early 19th centuries and advocated enamelling in colours (**324**), shallow engraving (**314**) and decoration at the furnace, for example trailing (**325**).

    During the last quarter of the 19th century the styles and techniques which were to influence the glass of the early 20th century became manifest in France in the work of Eugène Rousseau and Émile Gallé (**327**) from which the art nouveau (**328**) and then the art deco styles (**329, 330**) developed. Beginning in the 1940s there was a hiatus in the production of fine studio glass, though since 1960 an increasing number of studio glass-houses has been established (**332**) and a revival of the traditional methods of engraving has occurred (**333, 334**).

314

Given by the Friends of the Fitzwilliam.
Cf. Dudley, Dudley Art Gallery, *English 'Rock Crystal' Glass, 1878–1925* (1976).

316 FINGER BOWLS

English, late 19th century
a. Webb and Co.; stencil-etched with figures adapted from the Elgin marbles; etched on base 'Webb'. D: 12.5 cm. C.10.1976.
b. Acid-etched with 'Egyptian' motifs. D: 12.5 cm. C.3.1976.
The decoration on this bowl corresponds to that found on a suite of glasses in the trade catalogue of Gilbert Fleming, Wood Street, London, *c.* 1885, and called 'The Egyptian'.
Napier Duplicates Fund.

314 CARAFE

English, *c.* 1860
Acid-etched with underwater flora and fauna. H: 18.3 cm. C.2.1974.
Given by the Friends of the Fitzwilliam.
JGS XVIII (1976), p. 246 fig. 32.

315 'ROCK-CRYSTAL' VASE

English, second half of 19th century
Deep and shallow moulding; cut and engraved decoration. H: 30.3 cm. C.1.1974.

317 COVERED GOBLET

Bohemian, mid 19th century
Clear glass stained and overlaid with red; cut, and engraved with a forest scene. H: 45.3 cm. C.2.1977.
Napier Duplicates Fund.
Illustrated overleaf

318 GOBLET

English, probably by James Powell & Sons, Whitefriars, London, *c.* 1850.
Double-blown; interior silvered, exterior overlaid with green; cut, and engraved with the coats-

317

318

of-arms of the City of York and of the Dukes of Somerset; base inlaid with a seal marked 'E. Varnish & Co., London, Patent'. H: 22.9 cm. C.51.1972.

The Perceval Fund and the Victoria and Albert Grant-in-Aid Fund; ex-coll. Charles Handley-Read.

RA, *Victorian and Edwardian Decorative Arts: The Handley-Read Collection* (1972), pp. 17–18 no. A28.

319 VASE

Bohemian, mid 19th century
Clear glass overlaid with opaque-white; cut and gilded. H: 32.5 cm. C.1.1977.

Napier Duplicates Fund.

320 CLARET DECANTER AND STOPPER

English, *c.* 1898
Clear glass overlaid with green; cut, and mounted in silver marked for Birmingham, 1898. H: 45 cm. C.7.1970.

Given by L. M. Angus-Butterworth.

321 PAIR OF COVERED DISHES

Possibly Bohemian, mid 19th century
Yellow-green glass; moulded and cut. H: 15.5 cm. C.19a–b.1972.

Given by Colonel and Mrs Redvers Taylor.

322 FOOTED BOWL

English, late 19th century
Inverted bell bowl in clear glass with swags of green; clear hollow-knopped stem on rib-moulded

320

323

domed foot with green trailing at the edge. H: 25.6 cm. C.18.1977.
Napier Duplicates Fund.

323 OPAQUE-WHITE VASE AND COVER

Possibly English, 19th century
Enamelled in colours with floral motifs, and gilded. H: 32.8 cm. C.2.1939
Given by F. A. Lart.

324 THE 'WELL SPRING' CARAFE

English, glass by John Fell Christy, Stangate Glass Works, Lambeth, enamelled registration mark for 1847
Clear glass enamelled in greens and red with flowers and foliage; rim gilded. H: 15.9 cm. C.50.1972.
The Percival and V&A Grant-in-Aid Funds; ex-coll. C. Handley-Read.
Designed by Richard Redgrave, R.A. (1804–88) for Henry Cole's Summerly Art Manufacturers. RA, *Handley-Read*, A25; cf. H. Wakefield, *Nineteenth-Century British Glass* (London, 1961), pl. B.
Illustrated overleaf

325 GOBLET

English, James Powell of Whitefriars, c. 1876–1900
Light-green glass; vertical trailed decoration on bowl; hollow prunted stem; folded foot. H: 20.6 cm. C.9.1977.
Napier Duplicates Fund.
Illustrated overleaf

324

325

326 CLUTHA-TYPE VASE

Scottish or English, *c.* 1888

Bubbly green with streaks of aventurine.
H: 38 cm. C.13.1975.

Given by the Friends of the Fitzwilliam.

Clutha glass was designed by Christopher
Dresser and made by James Couper and Sons,
Glasgow. This vase, however, is probably an
imitation produced by Thomas Webb and Sons
under the name 'Old Roman'.

327 VASE

French, Émile Gallé, *c.* 1900

Blue, cased in orange and brown, and cut;
signed 'Gallé'. H: 28.3 cm. C.5.1977.

Napier Duplicates Fund.

See J. Bloch-Dermant, *L'Art du Verre en France,
1860–1914* (Lausanne, 1974), pp. 52–92.

327

328

328 CHALICE

English, James Powell and Sons, *c.* 1905
Light green; bowl engraved around rim
'REDDENS LAUDES DOMINO'; interior of
knop lined with blue foil; silver hallmarked for
London, 1905/6. H: 21.8 cm. C.12.1975.
Given by the Friends of the Fitzwilliam.
JGS XVIII (1976), p. 247 fig. 39.

329 VASE

French, René Lalique, *c.* 1932
Smoky-blue; engraved on the foot 'R.
LALIQUE . FRANCE'. H: 21.5 cm. C.6.1977.
Napier Duplicates Fund.
Cf. Haynes, *Glass*, pl. liia.

330 COUPE

Probably French, 1930s
Clear bowl overlaid with light green; opaque-
black knop and foot; rim ground. H: 12 cm.
C.17.1977.
Given by Professor and Mrs A. M. Jaffé.

329

334

332

331 SHALLOW DISH

English, possibly designed by Tom Hill of James Powell and Sons, *c.* 1935

Clear glass with wavy octagonal rim. D: 32.7 cm. C.5.1976.

Napier Duplicates Fund.

Cf. Honey, *Glass*, pl. lxx*b*.

332 DOUBLE-BLOWN VASE

American, Samuel Hermann, 1971

Yellow-green with splashes of metallic oxides; engraved on the base 'Samuel J. Hermann 1971'. H: 16.7 cm. C.17.1972.

Given by the Friends of the Fitzwilliam.

333 GOBLET, *The Bow Window*

English, diamond-stipple engraved by Laurence Whistler, dated 1972.

Clear glass; bucket bowl; ball knop with tear; conical folded foot H. 25.6 cm. C.18.1973.

Given by Miss D. Milton, to commemorate the directorship of Mr D. T. Piper.

JGS xvi (1974), p. 135 fig. 58.

334 PRESENTATION BOWL

English, Stuart and Co., engraved by David Peace, 1975

Etched with 'Stuart, England 1975', and with the trademark of the engraver; diamond-point engraved on the foot 'd. d. AMICI', and around the bowl with the signatures of those who presented the bowl to H. C. Hughes, M.A. F.R.I.B.A. H: 19.3 cm. C.6.1976.

Given by Mrs H. C. Hughes, in memory of her husband.

333

Published by the Syndics of the Cambridge University Press
The Pitt Building, Trumpington Street, Cambridge CB2 1RP
Bentley House, 200 Euston Road, London NW1 2DB
32 East 57th Street, New York, NY 10022, USA
296 Beaconsfield Parade, Middle Park, Melbourne 3206, Australia

First published 1978

Printed in Great Britain at the
University Press, Cambridge

ISBN 0 521 22008 4 hard covers
ISBN 0 521 29335 9 paperback

Library of Congress cataloguing in publication data
Cambridge. University. Fitzwilliam Museum.
Glass at the Fitzwilliam Museum.
Catalogue of an exhibition at the Fitzwilliam Museum.
1. Glassware – England – Cambridge – Exhibitions.
I. Title.
NK5101.5.G7C353   748.2'074'02659   77-27570
ISBN 0 521 22008 4 hard covers
ISBN 0 521 29335 9 paperback